R N/d

CAPTAINS
AND KINGS

by Oliver Warner

LIFE'S FEAST
letters: 1926

A SECRET OF THE MARSH
a story: 1927

HERO OF THE RESTORATION
biography: 1936

UNCLE LAWRENCE
a portrait: 1939

CHARLES THE FIRST

From a Miniature by David des Granges in the National Portrait Gallery:
a little known portrait of the hunted years shortly before his death

CAPTAINS
AND KINGS

a Group of
Miniatures

BY

OLIVER WARNER

LONDON
GEORGE ALLEN & UNWIN LTD

FIRST PUBLISHED IN 1947

PRODUCED IN COMPLETE COMFORMITY WITH
THE   AUTHORIZED   ECONOMY   STANDARDS

PRINTED IN GREAT BRITAIN
in 11-point Fournier type
BY UNWIN BROTHERS LIMITED
WOKING

TO
BRIDGET, CHARLES & OLIVIA

PREFACE

IT is the intention in this book to portray a group of people, some of whom were eminent in their day, many of whom have been forgotten. Since in all but a few cases, the information on which the portraits are based is readily accessible, they must stand or fall by the pleasure they may give to the general reader rather than to the historian. If it is the work of a life-time to become expert on a decade, no claim could possibly be made to authority upon so wide a field as is compassed herein.

The portraits (which sometimes overlap), fall roughly into three groups. First are Cromwellian. They derive from the accident of descent from Old Noll, an inheritance shared with many now living, but reinforced by familiarity from childhood with various personal possessions of the Protector, and with a collection of coins and medals of the period made with skill and learning by my father.

Naval interests next predominate, and here thanks are due to the Admiralty librarian and his ever courteous staff, who made it possible to study material not easily come upon at a time when great London collections were dispersed.

The last group is of soldiers, mainly Victorian; and a postscript has been included which, while in the form of fiction, is based upon a true incident. Opening with the last British sovereign to enjoy theology, the series closes upon the first to savour the delights of the motor-car. Between are bye-ways in biography over three centuries which, it is hoped, readers may be tempted to explore further for themselves. To this end a note has been included on some of the less well-known sources.

Various editors have been kind enough to allow the inclusion of material which originally appeared in their pages, although in each case this has been revised and sometimes re-written: acknowledgement is made to *Blackwoods Magazine*, the *Quarterly*, the *Army Quarterly*, *Time and Tide*, the *Contemporary Review*, the *National Review*, and the *English Review*, and, for the use of illustrations, to the authorities of the National Maritime Museum, Greenwich, the British Museum, and the National Portrait Gallery. Particular thanks are also due to Mr. John Stainer, who was so good as to supply little-known details of the life of Sir Richard Stayner; to Mr. Philip Unwin, who encouraged the present collection; to Mrs. Walter Bradshaw and to my father, who read my proofs.

CONTENTS

ILLUSTRATIONS

I

CHARLES: THE SHADOWS DEEPEN

ONE of the incidental delights of history lies in recalling the personal links between one age and another; in the thought, for instance, that Milton as a child may have seen Shakespeare; that Marlborough attended Monck's obsequies; that Hawke knew Nelson. But there seems a great gulf fixed between, say, the hopeful vigour of Elizabeth and the dark perplexities of the Civil War. In one England appears young and united, in the other sere and torn with question. Even so, there are links, vivid enough in their way. For instance, when Charles I was at Holmby, in that Indian summer of his reign when, having lost the war, he engaged in his not inconsiderable effort to win the peace, he was pleased sometimes to walk and jest with one of the Parliamentary Commissioners appointed to attend him. This was Philip, fourth Earl of Pembroke. Though grown old and stout and full of oaths, this was that same man, one of the "incomparable pair of brethren," to whom Shakespeare's First Folio was dedicated.

Pembroke was a substantial reminder of a greater age and of the greatest playwright, and considering that at least this one man played a part in the story both of Shakespeare and of Charles, (remembering, too, that the King was a reader of the Folio, annotating his copy), a fancy may well be provoked. What would Shakespeare himself have made of the highly complex drama unfolded within thirty years of his own death? Charles and his era, favourites as they have been in the theatre, have had to depend on far less gifted writers for presentation to posterity. Too often they have taken to the theme a bias or sentimentality to which it readily lends itself. That being so, perhaps it is permissible to guess at some of the facets with which Shakespeare would have been concerned had he lived to write "The Famous Tragedie of England's Commonwealth."

Seizing as he always did upon the mainspring of character, he would have perceived that Charles's faultless dignity covered a fatal defect; he was unwilling to keep faith with his fellowmen. His deception was deliberate. "Sovereign and subject are clean different things," he said on the scaffold, and it was among his deepest convictions. The effect was that he was trammelled by none of those fetters of conscience which afflict men of lesser station in keeping a difficult bargain. Although he toyed with others, the only kind of agreement he really understood was what the Germans call a *diktat*.

He had been beaten up and down the country in fair fight. The climax was reached at Naseby, where the New Model and the Cavaliers met in their last decisive clash. Afterwards it was a matter of time before even Oxford surrendered. The King fled to the Scots before the city was actually invested, and began that long process—extending over nearly three years and a second Civil War—which ended at the block. It was after he had left the Scots at Newcastle early in 1647 that the final act begins; one which, from the personal side, is perhaps the most enthralling. For Charles became a prisoner, his state varying from dalliance at Holmby and pomp at Hampton Court to the indignities of Carisbrooke and after.

Although he lost, it did not seem so until the very end. Appearances deceived. On his way to Holmby from New-castle the country people turned out to do him honour, and this they did even on his final journey. They knew him but as King, even though fallen upon misfortune. At Holmby, where he stayed until June, much seemed fair. The noble house, a royal possession, and a monument of the great days

14

of Sir Christopher Hatton, was itself a pleasant setting, though it lay close to the fatal field of Naseby. The Commissioners were courtesy itself. They played at bowls with him at Althorp or at Harrowden; forms of ceremony were observed; and although they interfered with those who attended him, Charles felt himself courted.

Then entered Cornet Joyce, who bore him away by force to army headquarters, a notable service accomplished with much adroitness: even the details have come down to posterity. One of them is that, of Joyce's whole party, the King himself appeared the most cheerful. At Newmarket, the destination, Charles found Fairfax. Once he had described him as "the rebel's new brutish general"; he now called him "a man of honour." Fairfax protested that the King had not been seized by his design. Charles smiled. The wheel of fortune was spinning in his favour. The army had him: their grandees now wooed him, Cromwell and Ireton among them. Cromwell was quickly enchanted. "The King," he declared in one of his generous outbursts, "was the uprightest and most conscientious man of his three Kingdoms." He saw him with his children; such felicities touched him nearly. Hitherto, his acquaintance had been at best remote.

There was, of course, a shadow. It fell first upon Cromwell and only later, though fatally, upon the King. Cromwell was playing a dangerous game in taking part in any sort of negotiation. The stakes were high; trust was essential. In order to gain a peaceful settlement of the Kingdom, Cromwell was risking the goodwill of the army. Parliament's was not in doubt; it had been forfeited by Joyce's seizure of the royal person, at Cromwell's instigation, so it was said. If the "Heads of Proposals," so ingeniously framed by Ireton, had been accepted by Charles, England would have had a constitutional monarchy nearly a century before she did, and Cromwell would have become, perhaps, Earl of Essex.

The time was riper than the King; for, perceiving himself courted on every hand, and being moved with state to his royal palace at Hampton Court, he began to grow great once more.

"You cannot do without me," he declared, with a rashness which even experience had not tempered. "You will fall to ruin if I do not sustain you."

"Your Majesty speaks," said the loyal Berkeley, "as if you had some secret strength and power that I do not know of; and since you have concealed it from me, I wish you had concealed it from these men too."

The King's attitude was bad enough. What was worse was the fact, revealed by intercepted letters, that he contemplated vengeance on the very people with whom he was negotiating. Even in his darkest hours, when the stress of war had brought him to that premature age caught by the artist des Granges in a haunting miniature, he still purposed to be absolute. *Dum spiro spero*: he wrote the motto in his copy of the Second Folio. But if he was to live, it was to be as King.

At this crucial time, when Cromwell and Ireton knew for a certainty that there was no hope in negotiation with Charles; that, in fact, further parley must lead to a silken rope at the hands of a restored King and mutiny among the soldiers they had led with such skill and glory, two very different figures, both Thomases, grow big upon the scene. Although worlds apart, each had a vivid role to play. One was surnamed Harrison, the other Herbert.

Cromwell, always a master of pawn-play, caused the King to fear assassination, and the hint came to him that it was Harrison who intended it. This was untrue; yet Harrison, the type of bold fanatic with which the army was then filled, was one who intended to see justice done—justice to those who had won the war, by God's grace as they believed —and who still, it seemed, lacked conviction that this would ever be fulfilled. Political reward appeared to them as hard to come by as their pay. Harrison and his like had always distrusted courtly negotiation, knowing by instinct what their superiors discovered by experience, that it was useless.

So Charles fled to Carisbrooke, there—in the months between November 1647 and September 1648—to spin the final web of intrigue which led to the second Civil War, to the abortive negotiations with Parliament at Newport, and to his own undoing. Harrison's shadow had fallen upon him. As if in compensation, Herbert had by now won that place in his affections which he was never afterwards to lose. His own brief and perfect *Memoirs* would have been richly drawn upon for the concluding scenes in "The Famous Tragedie."

Herbert makes no great name in history, but he was one of those quiet, balanced men of which it is largely if anonymously composed. He was related to Pembroke, and had joined the royal retinue with a few other private gentlemen at Newcastle. Seldom afterwards, by night or day, was he far from the King. His transparency of character as well as his political innocence made him acceptable to all parties as personal attendant.

Herbert, at the last, had a strange colleague, no less a man than the political theorist, Harrington, author of *Oceana* and the founder of the original Rota Club, though few Rotarians suspect it. He was a man bursting with ideas, many of which later bore political fruit in the United States of America, where his name has much honour. Familiar with courts, the friend of rulers, he was in theory opposed to monarchy, and in due time suffered for his views. Harrington, like Herbert, had a kinsman among the Parliamentary Commissioners, and had been taken into the King's service at Holmby. Like Herbert, who once wrote a narrative of life in Persia, he had travelled widely, and his conversation delighted Charles, except when he broached the subject of

Republicanism. Red-headed, always more brilliant than dis-creet, an injudicious conversation lost him his place at the King's side at the very time when Charles had most need of friends.

II

Twice the army seized the King: once by the hand of Joyce; once by that of Ralph Cobbett. Both occasions were dramatic, though it is the first which is chiefly remembered. Cobbett took him to Hurst Castle.

Hurst, in Hampshire, stands at the end of a long spit of shingle almost like a bowl on the end of a pipe-stem. It was built as a blockhouse by Henry VIII to guard the western entrance to the Solent, and, as Charles himself remarked, was among the meanest of his castles. Here he was confined for eighteen days in circumstances which—remembering him to have known his Shakespeare—must have sharply recalled that scene in Berkeley Castle where Richard solilo-quizes on the fate of Kings.

The setting was indeed macabre. Charles, by interposing his foot, had prevented Cobbett from entering his coach at Newport, but nothing could prevent the Colonel taking ship with him from Yarmouth, His Majesty being attended otherwise only by Herbert—who had ague—by Harrington, and by Mildmay, his carver. They took three hours over the passage to Hurst, where they were received by one Isaac Ewer, a man who, as Herbert remarks, was not un-suitable for such a charge. "His look was stern, his hair and large beard were black and bushy; he held a partizan in his hand, and (Switz like) had a great basket-hilt sword by his side; hardly could one see a man of more grim aspect, and no less robust and rude was his behaviour."

The season was winter, the place damp and foggy. Accom-modation was meagre, and exercise could only be had upon the spit of shingle which linked Hurst with the mainland.

Yet even here, while Herbert suffered from the "vaporous air," the King, walking with his usual vigour, delighted those about him, even including the uncouth Ewer.

Within the castle all was dark. Even at noon candles were needed, while at night Charles had his wax lamp set as usual in a silver basin. It was here one morning that Harrington, being in company with Ewer and other officers, let fall some expressions of admiration at the King's skill in the negotiations with the Commissioners at Newport. Harrington could not have made a less fortunate remark, since the army's express purpose was to remove the King from the chance of coming to an agreement with the two Houses. This time it meant to have the final word. He was at once taken up. Ewer and his fellows left the room, and when they returned, it was to dismiss him.

That same night Harrison re-entered the stage. At Hampton Court Charles had fled from a mere rumour of his intention. The next approach was at once closer and more sinister. Harrington had gone, and Charles, who was more apprehensive than was his wont, lay in an uneasy sleep. "About midnight," says Herbert, "there was an unusual noise that awakened the King." By the flickering light of the wax lamp he marvelled "to hear the Drawbridge let down at that unreasonable hour, and some horsemen enter, who being alighted, the rest of the night was in deep silence."

Early next day the King rang his silver bell and ordered Herbert to find who it was that was abroad so late. Herbert got the name from a friendly officer, and returned to the King. He was shocked to see how much the news discomposed him. "I am not afraid," said Charles at length, "but do you know this is the man who intended to assassinate me, as by letters I was informed, during the late Treaty? To my knowledge I never saw the Major, though I have heard oft of him, nor ever did him injury. . . ." "I trust in God," he added, "who is my Helper. I would not be surprised. This is a place fit for such a purpose. Herbert, I trust to your care; go again, and make further inquiry into his business."

Herbert learnt that Harrison was to bring the King to Windsor.

Harrison, as if sensing the prisoner's feelings towards him, or possibly being unwilling to be drawn by that charm which had fallen upon so many of his fellows, remained unseen. He stayed two nights at Hurst, and "when it was dark," says Herbert, "having given orders for the King's removal, returned from whence he came, without seeing the King, or speaking with any that attended His Majesty."

III

Harrison was indeed no murderer, at least in the usual meaning of the term, though he was tried and executed as such after the Restoration. In the meanwhile, before the immediate drama ended, there was a not unfitting exchange of courtesies between two brave men.

The route to Windsor led through Lyndhurst, Ringwood, and Romsey to Winchester, where at the King's entrance the Mayor and Aldermen of the city (notwithstanding the times) received him with dutiful respect. He was welcomed by many of lesser rank, some of whom came, Herbert relates, "to pray for his Enlargement and Happiness." Thence to Alton and along the hilly road to Farnham. On the way here Charles saw a smart troop drawn up, at its head an officer "gallantly mounted and armed; a Velvet Monteir was on his head, a new buff-coat upon his back, and a crimson scarf about his waist richly fringed; who as the King passed by with an easy pace (as delighted to see Men well hors'd and armed) the Captain gave the King a bow with his Head all *a-soldade*, which His Majesty requited. It was the first time the King saw that Captain."

When Charles had learnt from Herbert that it was Harrison he "viewed him more narrowly, and fixed his eyes so steadily upon him" as to make Harrison abashed. The King said "he looked like a soldier, and that his Aspect was good and . . . not such a one as was represented . . . having much judgment in faces . . . yet in that one may be deceived."

That night Charles lay in Farnham. "A little before supper," relates Herbert, "His Majesty standing by the fire in a large Parlour wainscoted, and in Discourse with the Mistress of the House . . . discovered Major Harrison at the far end of the room talking with another Officer; the King beckoned to him with his Hand to come nearer him, which he did with due Reverence. The King then taking him by his arm, drew him aside towards the Window, where, for half an hour or more they discoursed together."

Charles, taxing Harrison with what he had heard, was at once relieved of his suspicion, yet another soon arose; for Harrison told the King, what in substance he repeated at his own trial, that he held the law "equally obliging to great and small, and that Justice had no respect to Persons." Upon this, Charles broke off his conversation, though he sat down to supper in happier mood, "being all the time very pleasant, which was no small rejoicing to many there, to see him so cheerful in that Company, and in such a condition."

Thenceforth King and Major parted company, Charles to Windsor with the faithful Herbert, Harrison to his post. They met once again, during Charles's trial at Westminster. Harrison sat among his judges. His signature and that of Ewer were upon the death-warrant.

Nothing can dim the steadfast courage of Charles's final days. It found response in simple hearts throughout the length and breadth of his realm, the same who rejoiced at the return of his son eleven years later. With him a whole epoch of Kingship passed. For the time, nothing adequately replaced it. Harrison and his like enjoyed some years of influence and power, but they were uneasy. England was restless under the Saints. But when the pendulum swung back and the monarchy was restored, Harrison did not fly. He stood his trial fearlessly, declared that what had been done in 1649 had been done in the light of day, and met his ghastly end with a fortitude in keeping with his ardent spirit. To die for deep convictions is the privilege of all free men.

2

FAIRFAX AND MARVELL

O N May 27, 1642, Charles was at York. He had issued a Proclamation requiring all the freeholders and farmers of the county to meet him on Heyworth Moor in a week's time. Accordingly, a great concourse of people assembled that June day, the King himself being attended by a body of nobility, two troops of horse, and eight hundred foot soldiers, fully equipped. They were the nucleus of the cavalier army. Before riding round the moor to survey his subjects he delivered a speech which few could hear, and although he himself declared it a most cheerful occasion, there was much murmuring, confusion and noise, and His Majesty's reception, so observers have recorded, was mixed. It might well have been.

The Yorkshire freeholders had been among the first to suffer, both in their time and purses, through the exigencies of two abortive campaigns against the Scots. They had provided money, men, and horses; they had reaped humiliation. If few at Heyworth knew how thoroughly the bonds which linked the King and his Parliament were in fact severed, all realized that the state of England was approaching a crisis.

For the most part, the loyalty of the county, however it murmured, was not yet seriously shaken. The King might err, but he was still the man who had been the supreme source of authority for seventeen years, and was of the line of princes. They admired his small but elegant person; they were flattered by his presence in the northern capital; they were there at his bidding.

Among those who knew something of the true significance of the progress from London was a man of thirty, Sir Thomas Fairfax. He would one day be a landowner of substance. He had married the daughter of Lord de Vere, foremost commander of his time, and he was the son of a Member of Parliament who had kept his family informed of the tremendous events which had recently shaken Westminster. His purpose on the moor that day was not merely to obey the Proclamation, but to present a petition desiring the King to be reconciled with his Parliament. Only a simple man could have hoped for success; but he was representative of many.

Charles was difficult to approach. He was surrounded, as so often, by insolent courtiers, and when Fairfax and his kinsman, Sir William Fairfax of Steeton, tried to draw near him, they were ridden off by Lord Lindsey, or Lord Savile, or another. Being an obstinate man, Sir Thomas followed Charles round the moor, and at last succeeded in passing through the guard to the King's side, placing the petition on the pommel of his saddle. The King discourteously urged his horse forward, and Fairfax narrowly escaped being trodden under foot: but the thing was done, and Mr. Secretary Rushworth later wrote: "The House is much contented with Sir Thomas's noble carriage of Thursday last."

To the King the petition and he who presented it were of no consequence. Both were ignored; but for the first time, quite unaware of their destiny, the two men who were to be the opposing figureheads in the Civil War had met on their set courses. It was to Charles's disadvantage that he did not look closer.

As men, they were not wholly dissimilar, except in height and appearance. Both had dignity. Both were brave, limited, and lovers of the arts. Both were blessed in their private lives, and had the quality of attracting devotion. Both stammered, and hesitation was of their essential nature. Both, almost against nature, had great authority thrust upon them.

Charles, born a second son, and admirably fitted for that role, quickly assumed the divinity he deemed the equipment of a King, and turned it into a defence. Fairfax, pushed upwards by an ability for war, and by the situation of his own party, slipped, after a few brief and crowded years, into a life which might have suited his sovereign. In the world of affairs, events overwhelmed both men.

The "royal actor" has had an embarrassing scrutiny from his own and every age. Fairfax, by contrast, has endured a neglect which he accepted in his later life, but which has led to his qualities being forgotten. By a curious chance he bore the same nickname as the greatest servant Charles ever had— "Black Tom." Strafford's arose from fear, Fairfax's from affection. Like Strafford, Fairfax came of a proud and splendid county: but even Yorkshire has produced few nobler children.

After Heyworth, the clouds rapidly gathered. In a torment of division, men took sides, family against family, brother against brother. In no country in the world could civil war come so cruelly as in England; and upon the whole, no civil war has ever been so humanely conducted. There were blots and excesses, but these were recognized and deplored as such. Although ultimately won with ease by the New Model Army of Parliament, the earlier stages of the conflict went largely in the King's favour. The Fairfaxes, old Ferdinando, Black Tom's father (no warrior in battle, but stout for his cause), and his far abler son at first almost alone defied the sovereign in the north of England. Their resources were as small as their enterprise was great. They could embark on no large-scale offensive: they became inured to difficulty, disappointment, and even defeat, though a series of small but brilliant engagements in the wool towns of the West Riding showed what Thomas Fairfax would do with wider opportunities.

Slowly the years dragged on. 1643 was indeterminate. It saw the capture of Wakefield by Parliament, and then the defeat of Adwalton Moor. In 1644 the younger Fairfax's star was rising fast towards the victory of Marston Moor, where, though his own wing failed, and Ferdinando bolted, Thomas Fairfax personally played a valorous part. To his life's end he bore a scar across his face from this fight, which sealed the fate of the lands over which he had conducted his early campaigns.

1645 beheld Fairfax Commander-in-Chief of the New Model Army. There followed the victory of Naseby, in which, though much was owed to Cromwell, the General captured a royal standard with his own hand. That was the major battle of the English war. In the same year came the siege of Bristol and, in a letter to Prince Rupert, who held that city for the King, Fairfax clarified his private position. "Sir," he wrote, "the Crown of England is and will be where it ought to be; we fight to maintain it there. But the King, misled by evil councillors or through a seduced heart, hath left his Parliament, under God the best assurance of his Crown and Family: the maintaining of this schism is the ground of this unhappy war." The letter adds that the King should no longer be advised by "those of whom the law takes no notice," but by his Parliament, in which "he hears all his people at once advising."

This moderate letter, echo of the earlier petition, added just reproach to a Prince whose immediate family owed much to the affection of the people of England, and who had repaid it by rapine. Fairfax had himself experienced his first taste of war in the Low Countries, fighting in the Palatine interest, and his thrusts were such that Rupert did not attempt to answer them. As for the contents as a whole, they read sensibly enough to-day, stating as they do the position of a constitutional monarchist; but in the circumstances of 1645 Fairfax's statement was a severe oversimplification. The issues were nothing like so clear to the rank and file (let alone to Lieutenant-General Oliver Cromwell) as they were to the Commander-in-Chief. Nor did the events of the tormented five years which followed Bristol sensibly alter Fairfax's attitude, while it hardened the revolutionaries. Fairfax was still, at heart, a loyal man; but his loyalty was to a condition of monarchy and government which, though familiar to us now for centuries, scarcely then existed except in idea. Politically, he was lost.

Once the sword was in its scabbard, once the drums had ceased to beat and the talking began, Fairfax seemed bewildered. His eclipse was so gradual, so resisted by his friends and indeed by all the moderates, that it was scarcely apparent until much later. It came about after, not before, the King's death, in which Fairfax had taken a passive part, though there is reason to think that he was deceived into a belief that there would be a last-minute reprieve, and it is quite certain that he disapproved the act. He had indeed become a leader without power, and although there is small doubt that Cromwell would have continued to serve under him in the field, the fact remains that when Fairfax refused to invade Scotland before the Dunbar campaign, Cromwell not only assumed his place, but undertook one of the greatest of all his military exploits. His sun was in splendour.

Fairfax's active military career had ended with the close of the second civil war in 1648, when he took Colchester after a stubborn fight. A siege had begun his martial education—that of Bois-le-Duc, back in 1629—and a sadder siege ended it. Gradually, quietly, he faded altogether from the public eye. It is true that there were later appearances: an unsuccessful tiff with Cromwell over Buckingham, his rascal son-in-law; a dramatic appearance at the head of the Yorkshire gentlemen during Monck's march southward in 1660 to restore Parliament; a voyage to Holland to invite the return of Charles II; but the glory was gone. Ill-health, the gout and the stone, which had never been long absent, had him in their grip, and he found himself as out of sympathy as he was out of touch with the ideas fermenting in London.

Yet there *was* something more, and history, with that irony in which she so delights, hid it both from Fairfax, and even from the young man whose felicity he inspired. Indeed, it was left to generations far ahead to realize the full beauty of the lyric poetry of Andrew Marvell, which blossomed and owed so much to the congenial atmosphere of the Fairfax household. For about the year 1650, when Fairfax had gone into retirement among his Yorkshire acres, and was devoting himself to his books, his gardens, and to that study of antiquity in which he so delighted, he appointed Marvell, then a man of about thirty, tutor to his daughter Mary.

Although only nine years younger than the General, Marvell reverenced him this side idolatry; nor is it difficult to see why. The Fairfax household was a spacious oasis of learning and kindness in a world Marvell knew to be hard. Its master was one of the greatest soldiers of his age and an ardent Yorkshireman besides; Marvell, all his life, was devoted to his own county. Fairfax had European prestige; Milton had addressed a sonnet to him. He was a triumphant leader; he knew something of travel, and his character, despite its weaknesses, was as nearly without blemish as it could reasonably be. The difference between them was that Fairfax owed much, and Marvell little, to riches and heredity; that one was a brilliant, and the other a wretched, though per-severing poet; most important of all, Marvell was capable of growth as a writer, as a politician, and as a judge of character. In later years he looked back to his two years at Nunappleton with delight, though he learnt, in the great arena of Commonwealth and Restoration London, new and more difficult loyalties. But in those magic months of the early 50's, there were few clouds. The King was dead; and away in the distant north, peace, however uneasy in reality, had for the moment descended on the harassed land.

Marvell's early years are still much a mystery. He was the son of the headmaster of the Grammar School at Hull, who was a classical scholar, and an excellent preacher. Andrew inherited his scholarship, and added to it an appetite for travel and experience which took him, after a spell at Trinity College, Cambridge, through a great part of Europe, much of which he came to know well.

One of the chief effects of his travel and his education was to give him precisely what these gifts are supposed to bestow—though they do not always do so—breadth of mind. His lyric poems are remarkable not merely for their range of sympathy and allusion, but for their ambiguity; often this is tortuous. At other times, where the meaning is clearer, they give an extraordinary sense of detachment and nobility. The best example is of course the famous *Ode upon Cromwell's Return from Ireland*. Is any other literature capable of producing a poem which can be quoted with delight by adherents of both sides of a civil war? Neither Charles I nor Cromwell ever had a subtler poetic tribute. It is a poem about which, the more he reads it, and the better he becomes acquainted with the atmosphere and politics of the age in which it was written, the reader must grow not less but more enthusiastic. Of its kind, it is unique; and its kind is rare. Final curiosity: Cromwell returned from Ireland in 1650; the *Ode* was first known to the public in 1776—and the gap of more than a century had neither tarnished its freshness and beauty, nor had history, despite some small corrections in perspective, in any way altered the lovely balance of its content.

Yet it was not politics, but gardens, mowers, fauns, and music which were the background of Marvell's choicest lyrics. In the sustained poem *Upon Appleton House* there is the clank of armour in the background; even the flowers do honour to the martial fame of their master, still hot from the war, and with wounds as yet unhealed. But when this tribute is done there is more delicate work to follow:

> Annihilating all that's made
> To a green thought in a green shade,

as the most famous lines Marvell wrote felicitously put it. There is the very scent of grass and flowers in *Damon the Mower, On a Drop of Dew, The Coronet, The Mower's Song, The Garden, Upon the Hill and Grove at Bill-borow, Upon Appleton House*, with its little-quoted apostrophe to England:

> Oh Thou, that dear and happy Isle
> The Garden of the World ere while
> Thou Paradise of four Seas,
> Which Heaven planted us to please,
> But to exclude the World, did guard
> With watery if not flaming Sword.

Besides this greenery, there are the love lyrics: *To His Coy Mistress, The Fair Singer, Ametas and Thestylis*, and many another. There are his metaphysical poems, *A Dialogue between the Resolved Soul and Created Pleasure, A Dialogue between the Soul and Body*, to name but two, and his lovely *Musick's Empire*:

> First was the World as the great Cymbal made,
> Where Jarring Windes to infant Nature plaid,

which rivals in sweetness if not in comprehension Dryden's great song for St. Cecilia's Day.

Such a harvest of beauty was garnered in that tutorship that, to quote his own *Bermudas*, he

> . . . Apples plants of such a price
> No tree could ever bear them twice.

The shaft goes deep; for Marvell faded later into satire and into politics, less permanent things, and, like his young charge, the future Duchess of Buckingham, doomed to insult and neglect, he was never moved again to such sustained and varied pleasure. He had done enough to assure him the passionate devotion of men of diverse ages and walks of life.

It is never possible to say of any of Marvell's simplest

lyrics that it is this or that. There is always a secondary as well as a superficial content. In such a plain instance as:

> See how the Flowers as at Parade
> Under their Colours stand displaid:
> Each Regiment in order grows,
> That of the Tulip Pinke and Rose.

—there opens an elaborate and splendid compliment to Fairfax the soldier as well as Fairfax the gardener. It has indeed the simplest ambiguity. Some of the lesser-known poems pose problems which need, and have recently received, elaborate interpretation; for Marvell in his lyrics was one of the most complex voices of his age. Beside his, the works of, for instance, George Herbert and even the younger Milton sometimes seem quick of apprehension.

Marvell's character bears out this complexity. Associated as he was with Milton in a Commonwealth secretaryship, devoted to Cromwell, incorruptible in the sticky and tortuous intrigues of the Restoration, he was in his own day accounted among the Puritans. Certainly his devotion to his constituents at Hull, whose interests he served so long, and to whom he wrote so often and so painstakingly, speaks of him as one not akin to the fly-by-nights of the court of Charles II. Yet his poetry, the best of it, is of a more unbuttoned outlook. He seems, indeed, to have reversed the age's process. When with Fairfax, and later working in London under a Commonwealth Government, his private attitude seems to have been essentially romantic. When times changed laxly, Marvell, remembering his training and tradition—Hull was the first provincial town to close its gates to Charles I—seems to have taken a tighter grip on his principles. Age and bitterness had something to do with it no doubt. It speaks much for Charles II's famous tolerance that he respected him, and read and liked his verse, even when it was directed against himself, as it often was.

Although by no means all Marvell's finest lyric poetry

was written at Nunappleton, a great deal of it certainly was, and the whole of his later work may be said to owe much to those spacious, fruitful and reflective years. So casual and so belatedly was Marvell's work given to the world, that it is very possible that some of his best lyrics are lost for ever. We are indeed lucky to possess any. That they are now valued at their worth is well evidenced by the volume of modern study he has attracted. Fairfax, too, has at last come to recognition. He was good as a man, inspiring as a soldier, and as a patron, one of the luckiest men of his time. Nor was the luck undeserved; for his first act, after taking Oxford from the forces of the King, was to put a guard on the Bodleian, which he subsequently enriched with manuscripts.

What Clarendon insisted on calling the Great Rebellion was in itself a disaster; yet it had strange facets and compensations. It fermented ideas: a thousand. One thinks at random of the Diggers, with their advanced ideas on property; of Harrington's *Oceana* and his founding of the Rota Club, with its influence to be so long and widespread; of Clarendon himself; of Milton's pamphlets. Less weighty than these, yet of more immediate pleasure to our own age, must be recorded the poetry of Marvell as one of the brighter jewels of a twisted time, produced by that strange and happy partnership of general and tutor.

It is said that every century looks backward not to its immediate past, but to that which seems to bear most nearly on its own problems. In our own age, we find increasing sympathy with those tormented days when England, emerging from the throes of war, was at the same time wrestling, not conclusively perhaps, but fruitfully, with a new order of her own, one which had and has profound influence on her future, and on that of the civilized world. It is not possible to-day to read a life of any of the great figures of the Civil War without a glow of sympathy for their perplexities, and admiration for their courage and achievement. In Fairfax is seen the plain and honest man writ large, with his courage, his faith, and his failure. In Marvell is the intellectual, the man who will hand on the germ of that conflict which distressed his generation, clothed in language of immediate pleasure.

3

LITTLE GENERAL MONCK

I think the bringing up of his little army entirely out of
Scotland up to London was the best stratagem that is extant
in history.

HOBBES.

I

"OLD GEORGE" is what his soldiers called him, with
reasonable pride and affection; and indeed it has
been given to few men to lead armies so bloodlessly, and to still fewer to refuse the Crown of England.
Such was the fate of George Monck.

Monck was an Elizabethan, not literally, but by tradition,
and in the extraordinary circumstances of his life. He was
born at Torrington in Devon, in the early years of James I,
when the personalities of the sea adventurers—Drake,
Raleigh, Frobisher, and Hawkins—were living memories;
and he began his career in the colourful way which it was to
continue. He thrashed the under-sheriff of the county, and
was forced to leave England with haste and in silence.

The circumstances were as follows. Monck's father was
a man of ancient family but of impoverished estates, who
lived in a fashion which he could not afford, and was in
constant danger of being arrested for debt. It so happened
that when the boy George was seventeen, Charles I, then
in the year of his accession, was on a progress westward,
to speed Buckingham's expedition against the Spaniards.
Monck's father, like other gentlemen of the county, rode
out to meet his sovereign, only to be arrested, almost within
sight of the royal party, by the orders of this under-sheriff.
The insult was too much for young Monck. He dashed into

Exeter, which was then plague-stricken, did his duty faithfully, and was immediately smuggled away by friends to serve in the very expedition Charles had journeyed to see.

Such a fate, which was by no means unwelcome to a spirited younger son, decided his whole future. He became forthwith a soldier of fortune, one who took his profession more seriously than most men of his time, and in which he slowly rose to distinction.

Twice he served under the unhappy Buckingham, seeing the depths to which incompetence of organization could sink, rendering as distinguished service as he could, and afterwards joining the forces of the States-General to fight the Spaniards in the Low Countries. In these early years he made the acquaintance of many of the officers who, on one side or the other, were to become famous in the English civil wars. Not the least among them was Rupert of the Rhine, who in one fierce assault of a walled town is said to have served as a volunteer in Monck's company.

Monck was thirty before he left the service of the States-General, left in disgust at his treatment by the citizens of Dort, who were unwilling to leave to his personal execution the punishment of certain of his men who had been guilty of riot. He returned to an England already clouded by the first signs of the coming struggle between King and Parliament. There was no question where Monck's almost traditional sympathies lay. They were uninfluenced by any wider consideration, for he had small interest in politics.

He served Charles faithfully, first in the indecisive war against the Scots, saving some English guns with his infantry at the rout of Newburn Ford, and later under Ormond in Ireland against the Papist rebels. When divergence of loyalties became more marked, and Ormond required his officers to take an oath, Monck, always "tender of oaths," and seeing another though unintended slight towards his professional conduct, flatly refused, and returned to England

35

under escort, though with a warm recommendation from his commander.

The King was at pains to win the continued services of this sturdy but difficult soldier. He summoned him to Oxford, and there, at a personal interview, not only gained him completely, but gave him a command among his former Irish comrades, who were then investing Nantwich under Lord Byron. Monck rejoined them, and fought valiantly at their head against Fairfax. His luck was out. He found himself deserted, was captured by the parliamentary commander, and was committed to the Tower of London.

Monck was in the Tower nearly two years. He was poor, and almost forgotten. His brother once sent him fifty pounds, and the King a hundred, an extraordinary mark of favour from impoverished Oxford, while Rupert of the Rhine once tried to get him exchanged; but for the most part he was lonely and miserable, except when under pressure to change his allegiance. Parliament were not slow in their efforts to win a professional soldier of such experience, but Monck, for all his poverty, would not betray his King.

Even so, he was not idle. He contracted a friendship with his laundress, who was a staunch though secret royalist. She was married, but her husband had disappeared, and she was formally united to Monck a few years later. And while captive, Monck wrote a very sensible book of military *Observations*, which remained in manuscript until his death, the solitary printed edition appearing in 1671.

At last an opportunity offered to serve in Ireland once more against the Papists. An oath was required, and there was the usual difficulty, but Monck, submitting at last, found himself with an active command in Ulster. He was soon, if almost imperceptibly, involved not merely against the rebels but against Ormond's royalists. After severe fighting, in which he won much reputation, he was again captured, at Dundalk, and was sent to England with a safe conduct.

Here, at Milford Haven, he met Cromwell, then preparing for his Irish campaign. This meeting was highly significant. The two soldiers took an instant liking for one another; they were much of a temper, and until his death Monck was Cromwell's staunch adherent. Their King was dead; both men were patriots and veterans; both desired peace and a stable government; and both were in the habit of considering that the end justified the means.

When Cromwell returned from Ireland, he remembered Monck, and he gave him a regiment of infantry to serve in the Scots campaign. This regiment was afterwards to win undying laurels as the Coldstream Guards, and is the sole direct descendant in the British Army of Cromwell's New Model. Incidentally, no regiment of such fame takes its title from so small a place.

Under Cromwell, Monck fought against Leslie. He led the foot at Dunbar, and the result of that desperate victory was due much to his council and valour. After Dunbar, he helped to subdue the more important Scots fortresses, and he was then granted leave of absence to England on account of ill health.

Healed by the Bath waters, Monck was next ordered to Yarmouth, to superintend the fortifications of that town. He was then given a commission, together with Deane and Blake, to serve as a general-at-sea against the Dutch. It may seem to-day a strange proceeding to offer command at sea to a man with so little nautical experience that he used to order his line of battle to "Wheel to the right!" and to "Charge!"; but the fact remains that, by sheer valour and determination, Monck and Deane, in Blake's absence, defeated and killed Tromp in a bloody battle off the Flanders coast. They returned to Portsmouth to be acclaimed by the nation, and to find Oliver Cromwell Lord Protector of England.

After this first brief and glorious service at sea, Monck's influence lay in Scotland during the years which remained until his dramatic descent upon England in 1660. Cromwell rewarded him by the second most important post in his dominions; and from Dalkeith, after having subdued the royalist highlands in a masterly campaign, Monck ruled Scotland with a firmness and justice which pleased the whole nation, who were as content under him as they would have been under any government but "that of their lawful Prince." Monck's intelligence service was magnificent; it rivalled that of Thurloe at Whitehall. He listened to every shade of opinion, allowed no liberty of action, and brought his own small army to such a state of efficiency that it had no rival in Europe at the time of Cromwell's death. As a soldier he had known defeat, and had profited by it. As an administrator he seems from the first to have had talent. As a sailor he was brave and vigorous.

II

When Oliver Cromwell died, a contemporary remarked, "not a dog barks, so great a calm are we in." Edinburgh, like other cities, dutifully proclaimed Richard his son as Second Lord Protector. There was as little enthusiasm in the Scots capital as elsewhere for the event. "Old George for my money!" cried one soldier, and the sentiment in Monck's army was universal, for his men were devoted to him. He had led, fed, and served them well, and they trusted him to the hilt, as they were soon to show.

Monck had many temptations, now and henceforward, to assume an absolute power. He resisted them all. He offered his services to Richard, and, when Richard fell, to the attenuated remnant which sat in Whitehall and was known as the Rump Parliament. When the army, under the leadership of Lambert, attempted to coerce the Rump, Monck electrified England (who had overlooked his power), by declaring his intention of marching south to safeguard the authority of Parliament. To do this, it was necessary to secure Scotland, and to restrain such of his own officers as he suspected. of being disaffected. His actions were as prompt as they were uncompromising. They were completely successful, and he marched towards the Border at the head of a few thousand picked men.

The story of his march south is a great one. Lambert lay before him in strength. There were other leaders to be reckoned with, men like Fleetwood, and Fairfax, who was ready to raise a party for the King, and against whom, as a servant of Parliament, Monck would be forced to act. His advantage lay in his treasury, which was full. Lambert, who had no such resources, was compelled to put his men at free quarters, and, if the Scots army could only gain time, discontent might soon disperse the English forces.

Monck took up his headquarters at Coldstream, commanding one of the best fords over the Tweed. There, in the roughest quarters, and in bitter cold, he lay during the significant weeks which changed the English news from bad to good. First the fleet, and then the Irish army, expressed a guarded sympathy; then Fairfax sent him a message saying that all he aimed at was a free Parliament, such as had not been held for twenty years; finally, although he made tentative advances, there came the news that Lambert's men were deserting, and that Fleetwood's had "spit in his face."

At dawn on the first day of 1660, Monck's army began its advance towards London, at first knee deep in snow. It was a triumphant progress. Bells rang; the country people turned out in hundreds to cheer the troops, shouting for a free Parliament; bonfires blazed. At Newcastle, Monck met the City of London Sword-bearer, who told him that London was unrepresented in the Rump, and implored his help towards a representative assembly; at York he found that Lambert had disappeared, while Fairfax rode into the city on the same errand as the Sword-bearer. Regimenting the pick of Lambert's men, Monck continued south, and at last entered London in state, where for the first time he and his men found their welcome uncertain. The citizens had learned to distrust all soldiers.

Monck, still nominally the obedient servant of Parliament, was now in effect the master of England. The Rump, with incredible foolishness, provoked the city into a declaration of non-payment of taxes, and then ordered Monck to dismantle the gates and portcullises. Monck, raging, obeyed, while the citizens were torn between their horror at such an insult, and amazement at seeing troops which gave their commander such obedience. But when Parliament continued its vindictive attitude to the city, the General rebelled. By openly declaring for a free Parliament, he won the heart of London in a single afternoon. Rumps were roasted in the streets, and he and his men were the darlings of the hour.

When Parliament saw that he was earnest in intention, their republican souls quaked, for a free Parliament meant a restoration of the monarchy, and they knew it. First they pressed Monck to declare his own opinions, and then, when he remained adamantly silent, they offered him the supreme power. He replied that he had the fate of the Cromwell family clear in his memory, and that he regarded the suggestion as treason. How secret he was at this time is remarked by Mr. Arthur Bryant, who calls him "the most cautious man in the three kingdoms." How difficult he was to approach was declared by the royalist Lord Mordaunt, who cried in exasperation, "He is a black monk, and I cannot see through him"—and then sent a report to Charles that he was sure he was a republican!

Actually, unknown to Parliament, Monck was in communication with the King. He sent a messenger in the first instance because, as a patriot, he felt it his duty to warn Charles to leave Brussels, which was Spanish soil, lest he should be seized by that country and, in the event of a restoration, held to ransom. Charles took the hint with thanks and expectation, moving to Holland. If the master of England served him so at this time, it promised well for the future. Monck, he declared, could within reason command him anything. Monck replied by supporting the famous Declaration of Breda, the terms of which Charles accepted.

England was now witnessing the death-throes of the Commonwealth. The people were voting a royalist Parliament to Westminster, London echoed to old songs, and when the new Houses met, all was over bar the shouting, of which there was to be a good deal.

III

Charles II and Monck met on Dover beach; and Monck greeted his sovereign, to Charles's surprise and relief, with every mark of homage and affection. Monck with his army had kept the peace while England declared its will, but he still had power, did he so desire, to send the King on his travels again. Far from abusing that power, he was henceforward Charles's devoted subject. He served him as faithfully as it was his custom to serve any master who employed his sword and used him justly. Charles called him, now and henceforward, his "little father."

He dealt well by him. He made him Duke of Albemarle, confirmed his army command, and gave him the choice of any of the great offices of State. Characteristically, Monck chose the Mastership of the Horse, the patronage of which was sufficiently extensive for him to be able to reward many of his old friends. As a Privy Councillor, his voice was an honoured one for the remainder of his life, and his sense of justice led him to be on the whole a staunch helper of those whose late opinions now caused them danger.

Monck's services did not end with the Restoration. He disbanded the standing army with an efficiency acknowledged even by Pepys, who was never one of his warmer admirers. Men of all ranks were found employment, while certain regiments of Guards were retained for the King's protection, and to keep order in London. It was thus that, besides the Coldstreamers, the Grenadiers or King's Foot Guards were formed, and the regiments of Household Cavalry. They were recruited from among Monck's men, and their establishment gives him a just claim to be the first Commander of the British Army as it is known to-day.

Nor was his service confined to strictly military affairs. Throughout the time of the great plague, when the court had moved to Oxford, Monck and the aged Archbishop of Canterbury remained at their posts in Whitehall with a cold and lovely courage, administrating the affairs of the kingdom; and when the great fire broke out some years later, the King at once summoned Monck from the fleet, where he was then serving, to allay the panic. "Had the little general been in London," said one citizen, "such a disaster could never have arisen." Such was the feeling of the people towards the man who now seemed the embodiment of all that was best in the old regime.

Monck's later commands at sea were sadder than those of earlier days. The King hesitated to call upon him in his age, but when political and other considerations led him to relieve the Duke of York and the Earl of Sandwich, there was little choice left but to appoint the two veterans, Monck and Rupert of the Rhine, to take their place. Although they fought gallantly, they bought success dearly against de Ruyter, and at the end of the campaign had the humiliation of seeing their flagship, the *Royal Charles*, taken during the Dutch expedition up the Medway, where the ship lay temporarily dismantled. Thanks to Monck's personal example, the incompetence of the Admiralty was rectified before the end of the war, and de Ruyter had no further success, although the Dutch secured what seemed to Monck a humiliating peace.

Monck died in January 1670, on a cold morning just ten years after the start of his great advance to London. He met death in "high Roman fashion," sitting upright in his chair, with his officers about him. He lay in state for many weeks, and Charles himself, with real grief, took part in the magnificent funeral procession to Westminster Abbey.

IV

Monck is overlooked, while the memory of many lesser men has lingered. That he had his good fortune in his lifetime there is no question. He deserved anything his country could give, for it was his strength, his ability to act, and his superb dissimulation which prevented a further outbreak of civil war; while had his personal ambition outrun his patriotism and his desire that the people of England should by their own free will end a military despotism of which he himself was no mean part, there is no end to the mischief which he could have caused. A dukedom, the Garter, and a quarter of a million or so sterling were rewards for such benefits as no other single man could bestow.

His personal character was as shrewd and serene as his tastes were plain, and neither so simple nor so honest that he could not deceive with devastating effect, both in battle and in diplomacy. He loved money, and he acquired it. He loved soldiering, and he led a matchless small army. He had a high estimation of himself, and he was fully honoured. If his personality and opinions inclined more nearly to the parliamentarian than to the royalist type, he was a man of sense and humour, his inner self reflecting that apple complexion which he retained almost to the end.

The visitor to Westminster Abbey may see a hideous

monument to Monck, in Henry VII's Chapel. This was erected in 1720 by the will of his son Christopher, second and last Duke of Albemarle, who died of drink. A plain stone marks his actual resting-place, which is near to that of Queen Elizabeth.

Pepys wrote a most unwilling epitaph, which deserves to be quoted. "I know not how, the blockhead Albemarle hath strange luck to be loved: though he be (and every man must know it) the heaviest man in the world, but stout and honest for his country."

4

LAMBERT

The mind of Lambert was a machine wasted first by friction,
then by rust.

WHITAKER, History of Craven.

IT is always fascinating to speculate on the reason for a
man's most important choices in life, particularly those of
a man of action. The reason is sometimes a woman, and
never more often was it so than among the leaders of the
Commonwealth. Cromwell, Lambert, Ireton—to name but
three—each were strongly influenced by women. Cromwell
owed much to his mother; Ireton to his wife, who was
Cromwell's daughter Bridget; while Lambert's ambitious
spouse helped to bring him in sorrow to exile in Guernsey.

John Lambert's life was a tragedy. The face which looks
out upon the world from contemporary pictures is a memorable one—sensitive, graceful, attractive, above all, ambitious.
He was a gentleman of Yorkshire, "well born," as the
historian of Craven records, "well bred, little tinctured with
fanaticism, of a competent fortune, an excellent understanding, and even an elegant taste": on the face of it a
potential cavalier. His home was at Calton Hall, a house in
Kirkby Malham in the West Riding, and he was intended
originally for a lawyer, although his studies appear to have
been slight. He was born in 1619.

He was only twenty years old when he married Frances
Lister, the daughter of a neighbouring squire, Sir Thomas
Lister of Thornton in Craven, and it was through his wife
that his decision arose to take the side of Parliament. Frances
had a great friendship for the Assheton family, who for many
years had been wrangling with Charles I's most trusted

ecclesiast, Laud, who wished to break their lease of a valuable rectory. It is clear that Lambert shared his wife's antipathy to Laud, and at the very outbreak of the Civil War he became a captain of horse in the army of Ferdinando, Lord Fairfax, father of "Black Tom."

From the first, Lambert proved himself a brave and popular soldier. He served with distinction at the siege of Hull, at Nantwich, at Bradford, and at Marston Moor, where, although his own cavalry were routed by a charge of Lord Goring's royalists, he himself, with the younger Fairfax and five or six troopers, cut his way through the enemy and joined the victorious left wing under Cromwell. From Marston Moor until the time of the Commonwealth Lambert's fortunes rose steadily, until he became one of the most powerful leaders in the army. His "subtle and working brain" was behind Ireton in his many schemes for making the soldiers the dominant factor in the settlement of the kingdom. He became a commander of the army of the north; served with valour at Preston and Dunbar—where he and Monck were Cromwell's ablest lieutenants—and in 1651 at Worcester, besides lesser fights.

The war over, Lambert was handsomely rewarded by Parliament, one thousand pounds a year being settled upon him. He was offered the post of Lord-Lieutenant of Ireland. For this dignity he is said to have laid out "five thousand pounds for his own particular equipage," but as Parliament actually abolished the title of Deputy in 1652, and as Lambert was dissatisfied with any lesser office, he never crossed to Dublin, remaining in England as President of the Council of Officers of the Army. Honours still fell thick upon him. He was principal among those who offered Cromwell the Protectorship, sat in his Council of State, was styled "my Lord Lambert"—even Pepys refers to his wife as Lady Lambert long after the Restoration—was made Major-General, and a Baron of the Cinque Ports.

46

His quarrel with Cromwell, inevitable perhaps with so ambitious a man, arose over the question of kingship. Although prepared to suggest the assumption by Cromwell of the sovereign title, "to try him," he opposed the measure when it was actually raised in Parliament: for "no sooner did he perceive his willingness to have the crown than he became a malcontent, refusing to take the oath to be true and faithful to his highness." Cromwell resented Lambert's attitude, deprived him of many of his places, and allowed him to retire to his house at Wimbledon, where for the latter part of the Protectorship he lived in obscurity, devoting himself to horticulture and painting, for both of which he had a talent. "It must have been a bitter pill," says Noble, "as he lost his pay as a colonel of a regiment of horse, and another of foot, as major-general of the army, and ten pounds a day as a general, besides his salary as President of the Privy Council and Lord Warden of the Cinque Ports: but to keep him from revolting, he was allowed two thousand pounds per annum." Towards the end of his life Cromwell made some attempt at a reconciliation, received Lambert in London, and made much of him, while his wife, who is said to have had a partiality for the Protector, was equally well received. "Cromwell fell on his neck," runs a contemporary account, "kissed him, inquired of dear Johnny for his jewel (so he calls Mrs. Lambert) and for all his children by name." Nor had he long to wait for further opportunity of advancement. He had retained a strong if secret following in the army, and in 1658, upon Oliver's death, fortune made him her deepest curtsey.

In England, when Cromwell had gone, Lambert had no rival in ambition and ability. "I wish Lambert were dead," wrote a royalist agent, "for I find the army much devoted to him, but I cannot perceive that he is in any way to be reconciled to the King. So that 'tis no small danger that his reputation with the Army may thrust Dick Cromwell out of the saddle and yet not help the King into it." The speculation was accurate. Although Lambert gave initial lip-service to the Protector's son, Richard, he was soon restored to his former offices, and with his tool Fleetwood quickly dominated the councils of the army. The highest power was within his grasp: the dreams of a lifetime looked now as if they could be fulfilled. Frances Lambert might yet be the first lady in England.

Actually, the country was seething with royalist discontent, but the one serious outbreak, the rising by Sir George Booth and Lord Derby in the north midlands, was suppressed at a single blow by Lambert and a few picked regiments. Booth's rising was so farcical and so boldly countered that the leader himself escaped from the field of action disguised as a woman, only to be captured without a struggle and confined to the Tower. Lambert's position appeared impregnable; so impregnable that over-confidence led him into a series of errors so grave that the rest of his life presents a decline as astonishing as it was rapid. First he coerced the Parliament to his will (true to the Cromwellian tradition) by setting the army in opposition to it, and putting a force upon it; he then called upon Monck, in Scotland, to support the military party. Monck's reply was a thunderbolt, the possible force of which Lambert had completely overlooked. He had always disliked Lambert, with the dislike of the professional soldier for the successful amateur. Now at last was his chance to show who was the better strategist. Monck declared himself a faithful servant not of the army but of Parliament, whose commission he held, and he backed his words by securing Scotland behind him, and by moving a picked force to Coldstream, where, in the bitter winter of 1659, his men waited for Lambert's English forces to dissolve.

Monck's waiting game was right. His own treasury was full; Lambert's men, who now began to advance north,

The Duke of Albemarle
& his Duchess

MONCK AND HIS DUCHESS

From a contemporary print in the British Museum, about 1661

were at free quarters, were unpaid, and were highly unpopular. They dissolved. Monck began his march from the
Border on New Year's Day, 1660, and met with nothing
more alarming in his progress southward than the cheers of
the villagers as the disciplined ranks of his men passed by,
and the ringing of bells.

He reached London to perceive himself virtually master
of England. Knowing Lambert to be his most powerful
rival in the army, since Fleetwood's men had revolted, he
procured an order from the Rump for Lambert to surrender
himself upon surety; and as he was not able to comply with
the condition of a bond of twenty thousand pounds, he was
confined to the Tower. Pepys, as so often, had a pertinent
comment. In his *Diary* under March 7-8, 1659-60 he wrote:
"My Lord did seem to wonder much why Lambert was so
willing to be put into the Tower, and thinks he has some
design in it; but I think he is so poor that he cannot use
his liberty for debts, if he were at liberty; and so it is good
and better for him to be there, than anywhere else."

If confinement had its uses for the prisoner himself, it was
essential for Monck to keep Lambert harmless. Monck's
settlement of the country; the free election; and the secret
negotiations with the exiled King—all demanded freedom
from disturbance. But Lambert had good friends, and they
were active. Of them the staunchest was one Slingsby Bethell,
who was hard at work raising money and support for another
move. He had almost succeeded in raising enough when,
on April 11th, there came the news that Lambert had escaped.
This was accomplished with the aid of his laundress, who
impersonated him while the warder was going his rounds by
night. Lambert slipped from a window by a silken rope,
said to have been made for him by a lady, and found his
way down the river in the small boat which two friends had
in readiness for him. He was quick to raise men, but Monck,
thoroughly alarmed, and with the King's Commission now

in his pocket, was even quicker. Monck sent Colonel Richard Ingoldsby against Lambert from Suffolk, and by a series of forced marches Ingoldsby intercepted the rebels near Daventry. When the two forces met, Lambert's men were half-hearted as well as outnumbered. Devoted to their old leader, they yet knew well the general feeling in the country, and knew that their revolt was doomed. Troops began to desert to Ingoldsby, scarcely any shots were fired, and on April 22nd Lambert was again a prisoner. What might have been the outbreak of a new civil war ended in farce.

Poor Lambert actually attempted to fly the field, but Ingoldsby, better mounted, overtook him, and threatened to shoot. Lambert reined his horse. "Pray, my lord," he implored, "let me escape; what good will my life or perpetual imprisonment do you?" Ingoldsby was inexorable, for Monck's orders were not ambiguous. Lambert made one last attempt to gain Ingoldsby's sympathy by offering to help restore the regime of Richard Cromwell, Ingoldsby's kinsman. Knowing the part Lambert had taken during the interregnum, Ingoldsby smiled, and Lambert, his spirit gone, was taken back to London. As he passed Tyburn, he heard the assembled forces drawn up near that place shouting for Monck and the King. His own designs and the hopes of his wife were for ever shattered.

Lambert had always been a dangerous as well as an able man, and it was scarcely surprising that he should have suffered severely at the hands of the new royalist Parliament. Although he was not present at the trial of the King—"through cunning or his own good fortune, he commanded at the siege of Pontefract during the time of the King's trial," Whitaker acidly records—he was eventually excepted from the Act of Indemnity, and stood his trial on June 9, 1661. In striking contrast to the fiery, unrepentant and courageous republican Vane, Lambert's deportment was so meek at this trial that he escaped lightly. He pleaded ignorance of the real intentions of Booth and Monck to restore the King, protested his loyalty, and was rewarded by the lighter sentence of perpetual confinement, to be suffered in the Isle of Guernsey. Even escaping death, he may be accounted unfortunate. Unlike Monck, unlike even Ingoldsby, who was a regicide, he had refused secret negotiation with the royalists, in the natural hope that he had more to gain by adhering to republican principles. "Had he accepted His Majesty's proposal sent by Lord Halton just preceding the Restoration," says Noble, "he would have secured a pardon, and received an ample reward." Even higher honours were at one time offered by the royalists, when it was feared that Lambert would make himself dictator. Lord Mordaunt proposed a match between the Duke of York and Lambert's daughter, while Lord Halton suggested that the King should marry her himself! His ambition, always stronger than his discretion, had betrayed him completely at last, though his conduct had more honesty than that either of the worldly Monck or the unprincipled Ingoldsby.

After 1661 Lambert disappears from history, save for an occasional sad glimpse. He was taken to Guernsey, where once again he employed his enforced idleness with horticulture—the King had indeed chosen well for him—"collecting the finest flowers that could be procured, and superintending the management of them." While in Guernsey he is said to have refused tempting offers for his services made by Louis XIV; but the history of his life in the island is so scanty that Whitaker records that inquiries made ninety years after his death revealed no tradition whatever of his life and dwelling. Lord Hatton, the Governor, was empowered to give him "Such liberty and indulgence within the precincts of the island as will consist with the liberty of his person." Between the time of the Restoration and of his trial he had already resided in Guernsey, where he had been allowed to take a house for his family. His relations with the Governor were not improved by a clandestine marriage between his daughter and Hatton's son; while in 1666, a plot for his escape having been discovered, he was for a time closely confined. Even now he was not left entirely in peace. Mrs. Aphra Benn wrote a lively play—*The Roundheads, or The Good old Cause*—lampooning his ambitions and, more particularly, those of his wife; while in later years Titus Oates accused him of a part in the Popish plot, though "with so little of an air of truth that even the court was not hardy enough to believe, or pretend to believe it."

It was long believed that Lambert died in Guernsey, but the discovery of *Plimmouth Memories*, collected by James Young in 1684, showed the following entries concerning the Island of St. Nicholas, or Drake's Island, near the entrance to Plymouth Harbour: "1667. Lambert the arch-rebel brought to this island . . . 1683. Easter Day. Lambert that olde rebell dyed this winter on Plimmouth Island where he had been prisoner fifteen years and more." Poor Lambert, his high ambitions reduced to the survey of a little island! Even with the consolation of his flowers and of his paintings, which were good, according to contemporary judgment, but of which there is now no trace, his mind and his memory decayed some years before his death, and his brilliant, thwarted life ended in the most tragic of all obscurities.

Lambert was not only a good and brave soldier, he was a man of wide interests. He is credited with introducing the Guernsey lily into England, and his taste for art led him to buy "divers rare pictures" that had belonged to Charles I. Charles II granted his ancestral estates to Lord Bellasis in trust for Mrs. Lambert, and they were inherited by his son John, who, like his father, was an "exact limner." John died in 1701, being at his death Sheriff of Yorkshire; so that in two lifetimes the wheel came full circle, and fate was once more kind to the Yorkshire family.

5

THE REGICIDES

IN 1798, while Napoleon was dreaming of the conquest of India through his expedition to Egypt, a country clergyman with a taste for parallels published the only history of the English regicides. Mark Noble, the cleric in question, Rector of Barming in Kent, and domestic chaplain to the Earl of Leicester, had been bred to the law, but he had sought a quieter living within the Anglican fold. He had already produced one work which remains a monument of embracing sweep, of assiduously collected gossip, of detailed inaccuracy, and shrewd portraits—his *Memoirs of the Protectorate House of Cromwell*.

His Dedication is of a piece with the whole. It is addressed to the regicides of France. "Gentlemen," begins Noble ironically: "You have copied the worst transaction recorded in our annals; and have the supreme infamy of having far exceeded those whose lives are here given. Preparatory to the murder of your own gracious sovereign, you printed the mock trial of our unhappy monarch. You will now also see, as a prelude to your own fate, that of King Charles I's judges."

Noble, so the reader feels, is fascinated by his subjects, just as he had been by Cromwell, fascinated in the way which horror always produces. His reproofs are as reiterated as they are pious; but it is his curiosity which makes him readable after a hundred and fifty years. He was not insatiable, for he would seldom pursue a fact until he had finally nailed it, but his net was wide enough. His work enshrines stories and opinions valuable as much as an illumination of his own day as of those upon which he was engaged.

Needless to say, public opinion in the late eighteenth

century roundly condemned the men who had put their King Charles to death. The time was yet to come when the act would find learned justifiers; while in our own day, we have seen scholarly opinion again swing slowly round in the King's favour.

Yet when the regicides are considered, one fact about them must always have stood clear: in the main they were brave men. They had the courage not merely to pass an illegal sentence, but to set their hand and seal upon their work. They did not represent the people; and their court, formed at the order of a purged Parliament, was no centre of justice; nor was President Bradshaw a lawyer of high skill or eminence. This they knew; but they also saw no other way of settling the government. They were called murderers eleven years later, but theirs was no hole-and-corner butchery. Other English kings had been dealt darker and crueler deaths than that which Charles met so calmly in 1649. Indeed the physical aspect of his martyrdom pales before the barbarous sentence passed upon his judges, the details of which are unprintable.

Thousands walk the world to-day bearing in their veins the blood of regicides, for no less than fifty-nine signed their names beneath the warrant for the King's execution, many of them family men. Their after-fate was so divergent that it is surprising it has caused so little research. It varied almost as much as their characters, their breeding, and their position in the State. It ranged from the bloody execution which overtook a handful of their number, through varying terms of disgrace and imprisonment to the honour enjoyed by Dick Ingoldsby. This man, a dashing soldier, swore that his hand had been forced by Cromwell. He further pleaded his activity against Lambert. He was given the Knighthood of the Bath at Charles II's coronation, and lived as the respected Member for Aylesbury until the last year of his new master's reign.

Ingoldsby had singular luck. Richard Cromwell said that though he could neither pray nor preach, he preferred him to all his other councillors. His very lightness of demeanour was probably his salvation. But others were of sterner stuff. Those who brought no repentance to their trial could expect no mercy. Meekness saved several from the gallows: friends at court saved others. One, Haslerig, excepted from pardon though not a signatory, had his life preserved for twopence. He enclosed it in a letter to Monck from the Tower which is still extant, reminding him of an earlier joking promise. He was spared only to die of illness a month or so later, still confined.

There was, in truth, little reason in the whole matter of punishment, though a verbatim report of the proceedings at the trial shows that there was at least a formal effort to be fair, during sessions at which drama, execration, and pathos are strangely mingled. But no stronger word than formal is permissible. The prisoners were granted no counsel. They defended themselves like rats in a corner.

The Act of Oblivion of 1660 covered all whom Parliament did not except, and in the resurgent flood of royalism several old scores were wiped off. One sufferer whose name does not appear on the warrant was Hugh Peters, a fanatic revolutionary preacher, "the most infamous reptile," says Noble, "that ever pretended to be a preacher of the Gospel"; another, though dying later, and in differing circumstances, was that able political visionary, Sir Henry Vane. There was also the sad case of the gallant Colonel Hacker, charged with the actual business on the scaffold, an executive obeying orders when others quailed. He seemed unable to assume the necessary penitence; made no formal defence and, alas, received no mercy. Of all concerned with the deed his fate must seem most hard. "Truly, my Lord," he said at his trial, "I have no more to say for myself but that I was a soldier and under command, and what I did was by that

Commission you have read." It must have added to his hurt that Colonels Huncks and Thomlinson, fellow guardians, gave evidence against him, going free themselves, as did Colonel Phayre, who was lucky enough to have married a daughter of Sir Thomas Herbert.

Eleven years is a long time to carry the memory of details: and it was largely details which counted in the post-Restoration trials. On the whole it may be said that the butchery was small. Charles II was, in truth, a more tolerant and understanding man than his unhappy father. It is always remembered against him that the corpses of Cromwell, Bradshaw and others were rudely hauled from their graves, but, however macabre, it is surely better to execute revenge upon a dead than a living man.

Of the fifteen signatories who died before the Restoration not all were disturbed in their graves. Six of the remaining forty-four were executed and one, Livesey, was murdered in Holland in 1660. Three more, Barkstead, Okey, and Corbet, were extradited and done to death in 1662. Lisle was murdered at Lausanne in 1664; and in the same year Hewson died of starvation at Rouen. Lisle's death found a horrid echo many years later, when his widow, Alice, came before Judge Jefferies for sheltering some victims of Monmouth's rebellion. She was beheaded at Winchester in 1685, victim of as brutal a death as ever a judge contrived. She harboured the men quite innocent of the character of their offence; and had he had his way Jefferies would have burnt her at the stake.

John Cook, the King's prosecutor, was tried with the main batch, as were two officers of the court, Axtel and Hacker. From his known opinions Axtel's name might well have been upon the warrant, but he pleaded with much justice that there were men on the bench before him loaded with as much crime. Cook, the professional lawyer, displayed a wonderful defensive barrage of words, though they were useless. Sir Hardress Waller, taking a leap in the dark, pleaded guilty, and was allowed to remain in prison until his death.

Thomas Harrison, the first regicide to die (on October 13, 1660), was a good soldier and an ardent fifth-monarchy man. It was not long before Venner, a wine-cooper, led these same fifth-monarchists to a serious insurrection in the City of London, and authority already had reason to be scared of them. Harrison comforted his wife by telling her he would "come again in three days." John Carew, of the same persuasion, died with a similar optimism two days later.

Next day followed John Cook and Hugh Peters. Cook was a sincere penitent, Peters a craven who died amid general contempt. He was a man who had, and deserved, few friends. The people knew him for "a snivelling preacher." On October 17th died Thomas Scot, Gregory Clement, Adrian Scroop, and John Jones. Scot had at one time been wholly unrepentant, and wished no better epitaph than that he "had a hand and a heart in the execution of Charles Stuart." He declared this in Parliament, shortly before the return of the monarchy. It is not difficult to respect him.

Clement, penitent, prayed for the reigning King, as did Scroop and Jones, who had married Cromwell's sister. Scroop was much pitied "as in regard he was a comely person." He was of good family, indeed, as Noble records, the head of it, Sir Gervase Scroop, fought with the royalists at Edgehill, and was wounded in sixteen places.

Many judges, fleeing the country, altogether escaped retribution. Three, Whalley—cousin to Cromwell—Gosse, and Dixwell, discovered a kinder haven in New England than in old, the first two sailing at the last moment possible on a ship well named the *Prudent Mary*. In 1794 they found a biographer in Ezra Stiles, President of Yale, who published a long account of their escape, life, and death. Whalley and Gosse in particular had many adventures, living for some time as troglodytes, while Dixwell lasted in comparative peace to 1689, just missing the arrival of news of the English revolution. Others died in prison, among them the lecherous Henry Martin "with food in his mouth," says Noble, "in 1681, and in the seventy-eighth year of his age." He was lodged in Chepstow Castle some twenty years, and there is a story told of him that he was used to rest in a cottage on his daily exercise, a privilege he forfeited when its owner asked him if he yet repented, and was given a stout denial.

Greatest of all escaping regicides was Edmund Ludlow. If not an amiable character, he was at once forcible and enterprising. Like many of his colleagues, he disapproved as much of Cromwell as of Charles, and at the Restoration, reckoning nothing of the promise of princes, fled to Switzerland, in whose austere mountains he found a refuge which lasted over thirty years. He is buried at Vevey, where he died in 1692.

Like other retired soldiers before and since, he wrote his memoirs. These, though strongly coloured, are one of the most valuable source-books of their age; and their spirit breathes neither meekness nor repentance. Having seen the death of Charles II and the exile of his brother James, Ludlow, thinking that old scores must be now surely forgotten, appeared in the fleet of William of Orange to assist in the siege of Londonderry. William, though he had little kindness for the memory of Charles I, could not stomach the appearance of a regicide. He sent him a message to return, or he would be seized.

With his stern spirit passed the last of those who killed their King.

6

THOMAS HARRISON

I

POPULAR feeling may start a revolution, but when once the wheels begin to turn they race. Then, when out of control, masterful minds grapple and at last make them run to their own direction. The plain man, who began with grievances about which he was moved to fight, finds himself under a worse tyranny than ever, though a new one. Three courses may be open to him: he may acquiesce, solacing himself with hope; he may fly; or he may fight underground. Very roughly, that is what happened after the death of Charles I. Most acquiesced because they were weary or tied to their homes; a few fled with the court; while others, little encouraged by success, became secret agents or what might now go under the term Fifth Columnists. As for those who seized government, it happened that they were headed by a conservative man of genius, or chaos would have resulted. Even as it was, Cromwell suffered from the usurper's customary lack of trained administrators, and had to use what material lay to his hand, if he could. Some of it was intractable.

Thomas Harrison was a prime example. Like many Puritan leaders he was of obscure birth, and was a true fanatic. He fought bravely, always in a spirit of zeal which made him the pattern of an Ironside. He was in the forefront at the King's trial, and it might have been supposed that political upheaval would have brought him content. It did not—he was happier fighting. He was soon in trouble with the new powers, and was for some time in confinement for complicity in plots. He may be acquitted of worldly ambition,

59

for had he acquiesced, Cromwell would have made the fullest use of him. Harrison's hope was of another kind. He looked for the rule of the Saints. He fought underground, though on the celestial side.

When retribution came, he was among the first victims. It was nothing that he had been little use in Cromwell's later years. He was known for a subvertor of established conditions. That was enough.

II

It is impossible to doubt the fervour with which the Restoration was greeted, even though the ironic new King was astonished by it. The same popular pressure which had started the wheels of change now impelled them to an ancient highway. It is notable, too, that the directing agency was military, while the speed and smoothness of events caused general surprise.

It was, perhaps, impossible that retribution should be avoided, but it took eccentric form.

The court which assembled at the Sessions House in the Old Bailey to try the regicides was of impressive composition. The returned royalist grandees were there, Clarendon, Southampton, Ormond, Somerset, Berkshire, Dorset, sitting with the Lord Mayor and most of the legal eminence in the country. With them were two odd figures, Monck and the Earl of Manchester.

The atmosphere was more than solemn, it was religious. Fortunately a scribe took notes, and the scene has come down to us almost complete. Many on the bench were uneasy, as well they might be, for the Lord Chief Baron made it clear enough, in a long, ferocious, and closely argued speech, the monstrosity of those acts of treason done so long before. The compass of retribution might be narrow but it must be clear.

Of Harrison's condition at the trial we also know something. He was over fifty. He had been imprisoned more than once, and of late closely guarded. He had been wounded often in the wars, and his limbs sometimes shook from the effects. The court wanted contrition. It had it in full measure from Sir Hardress Waller, who after natural hesitation pleaded guilty, and escaped with punishment for life. Other regicides also expressed sorrow.

Harrison was of sterner stuff. At first he refused to plead, wishing to be tried not "by God and the Country," but "According to the Laws of the Lord." He challenged those summoned for the jury up to the full number allowed, which was thirty-five, and when the case opened, defended his actions with a courage which, remembering him to have had no counsel, to have come straight from the cells, and to have been faced with such judges, compels respect. "My lords," he said truly, "the matter that hath been offered to you was not a thing done in a corner. . . . What was done was done in the name of the Parliament of England, . . . and whereas it hath been said we did assume and usurp an authority, I say this was done rather in the Fear of the Lord."

This was too much for the court, particularly as Harrison had had the face to add: "You know what a contest hath been in these nations for many years. Divers of those, that sit upon the bench, were formerly as active . . ."—the sentence was not allowed to continue, nor was Harrison's appeal to the nation. "You are mistaken," said the prosecution, "if you appeal to your countrymen. They will cry out, and shame you."

"Maybe so, my lords, some will," came the retort, "but I am sure others will not."

Harrison's version of his personal bearing towards the King is confirmed by others. Private animosity was absent: zeal for what he considered justice on the ruler who had "set up his Standard against the people," certainly was not.

"I would have abhorred to have brought him to account," he said, "had not the blood of Englishmen been shed."

The court suffered his defence with little patience; it is a wonder that he was heard at all. The verdict could not be in doubt, and the details of the death sentence were of such barbarity as to recall that this was indeed the century of the Thirty Years War. Though Harrison had no counsel, it should be recorded that just one sentence was spoken from the bench on his behalf. This came from the Earl of Manchester, one who had held command in the field for Parliament, and in whose regiment Harrison had served. "I beseech you, my lords," said this unhappy peer, "let us go some other way to work." No one took the faintest notice.

Harrison, with a handful of others, died, as some thought, a martyr's death for an example to traitors. Though his limbs indeed shook on the scaffold, his courage did not desert him, and if sacrifice was necessary, the choice was appropriate. He was no waverer. His constancy was of a kind only possible in the deeply religious or at least the deeply convinced. His whole life, with its passion and its errors, was lived by the fierce light of his conscience. The sincerity of his beliefs none could question, though they were not of a kind which made them acceptable to the ordinary man. One such, an acquiescent, saw with his own eyes the final scene of the drama. It was October 13, 1660, a day suitable enough. "I went out," says Pepys, "to see Major-General Harrison hanged, drawn and quartered . . . he looking as cheerful as any man could do in that condition. . . . Thus it was my chance to see the King beheaded at White Hall, and to see the first blood shed in revenge for the King at Charing Cross."

7

TWO HEADS:
CROMWELL AND THE KING

CLEARER brains than that of the celebrated Mr. Dick have been bemused over King Charles's head, and by an odd fate neither Charles nor Cromwell, linked otherwise so cruelly by fate in life, were in death suffered to lie in peace.

There are two accounts, one by Clarendon, the other by Thomas Herbert, of how Charles was buried. Herbert's is much the fuller, and was written from direct knowledge of the events described. After the execution, according to Herbert, the royal body was immediately coffined, covered with a velvet pall, and carried into the Banqueting House at Whitehall, there to be embalmed. It was then re-coffined, cased in lead, and removed to St. James's. "Where to bury the King," says the narrator, "was the last duty remaining." As Charles had spoken nothing of his wishes on this subject, either to Herbert or to Bishop Juxon, who attended him on the scaffold, Herbert made application for his internment in the Chapel of King Henry VII in Westminster Abbey, but was told, "Burying there would attract infinite numbers of people of all sorts which . . . as the times then were, was judged unsafe and inconvenient." Herbert and the Bishop then asked leave to bury him in St. George's Chapel, Windsor, and this was granted, after some deliberation, on February 6, 1649. The Parliamentary Governor of Windsor was ordered to observe the ceremony.

On February 7th the corpse was taken from London in a conveyance drawn by six horses, accompanied by about a dozen gentlemen. At Windsor, Colonel Whitchcot, the Governor, was shown the order for burial: meanwhile, the coffin was placed in the King's usual bedchamber, within the castle. Herbert and others were for placing the King's body in the vault of Edward IV, founder of the Chapel, but upon the arrival of Juxon, together with some noblemen, their choice was over-ruled. "One of the Lords beating gently upon the pavement with his staff, perceived a hollow sound; and thereupon ordering the stones and earth to be removed, they discovered a descent into a vault, where two coffins were laid near to one another, the one very large, of an antique form, and the other little. These they supposed to be the bodies of King Henry VIII and Queen Jane Seymour his third wife, as indeed they were. The velvet palls that covered these coffins seemed fresh, though they had lain there above one hundred years."

In this place they decided to bury the King, having inscribed the coffin in "capital letters of lead" with these words only: "King Charles, 1648"—the date being according to the old reckoning. As the coffin was borne from the castle it began to snow, "and the snow fell so fast, that by the time the corpse came to the west end of the Royal Chapel, the black velvet pall was all white (the colour of innocency), being thick covered. . . . Thus went the White King to his grave." Colonel Whitchcot would not allow the Bishop to read the burial service as set forth in the Book of Common Prayer, while a foot-soldier, "greedy of prey," had taken the opportunity, before King Charles's coffin was carried to the vault, of cutting "so much of the velvet pall that covered the great body" (that of Henry VIII) "as he judged would hardly be missed." He had also "wimbled a hole through the said coffin" and extracted a bone.

Having at last set the master whom they had served so faithfully to rest (in dignity and peace as they must all have thought) the little group of cavaliers dispersed. They had wrought indeed better than they knew, for the body lay undisturbed for the better part of two centuries. This, however, was not altogether purposed, for some twelve years later, after the Restoration, it was wished to bury Charles in greater state. It might be supposed that the resting-place would have been found without much difficulty, but the chapel had been thrown into such disorder during the time of the Commonwealth that two of the noblemen who had been present at the original burial, Southampton and Lindsay, who visited Windsor by order of Charles II to rediscover the vault, "could not satisfy themselves in what place or part of the church the Royal body was interred." If the resurgent royalists were thwarted of paying this last mark of respect, they could at least wreak delayed vengeance on the poor remains of his enemies, principally Cromwell, Ireton, and Bradshaw. They were dragged from their tombs to Tyburn, there to suffer those ghoulish indignities which can certainly have been no pleasure to Charles II.

Even this was not the end of the matter, either for Charles or for Cromwell. Early in the nineteenth century, during the building of a mausoleum in St. George's Chapel, "an aperture was made accidentally in one of the walls of the vault of King Henry VIII, through which the workmen were enabled to see, not only the two coffins which were supposed to contain the bodies of King Henry VIII and Queen Jane Seymour, but a third also, covered with a black velvet pall, which . . . might fairly be presumed to hold the remains of King Charles I." The words are those of Sir Henry Halford, physician to the Prince Regent. Halford was responsible for the first authentic account of the rediscovery of the tomb, and was present when it was proved beyond doubt that it did indeed contain the body of King Charles.

The Regent, who had a taste for history, ordered the vault to be thoroughly examined. On April 1, 1813, attended by the Duke of Cumberland, the Dean of Windsor, and a few

E

other witnesses, he himself visited the place, guaranteeing by his presence that "the most respectful care and attention to the remains of the dead" should be observed. Preceded by a castle servant with a light, the Prince, according to another account, by Frith the painter, entered the vault and ordered a master-carpenter to "open the coffin, and be very careful how you do it." There on the top was the simple inscription of Herbert's narrative, in large, legible characters on the scroll of lead. A square opening was made in the upper part of the lid, which revealed an internal wooden coffin, very much decayed, "the body carefully wrapped up in cere-cloth."

This cloth was removed with some difficulty, and, says Halford, "the whole face was disengaged from its covering. The complexion of the skin of it was dark and discoloured. The forehead and temples had lost little or nothing of their muscular substance; the cartilage of the nose was gone; but the left eye, in the first moment of exposure, was open and full, though it vanished almost immediately; and the pointed beard, so characteristic of the period of the reign of King Charles, was perfect. The shape of the face was a long oval." Round the throat was a piece of black ribbon. Mercifully, perhaps, the camera had not then been invented, but a sketch was made of the head, and is appended to Halford's account. This evidence, and the first-hand account heard by Frith from a witness present, then a young boy, apprentice to the carpenter, leave little doubt as to the extraordinary accuracy of Vandyke's pictures. The carpenter was next ordered to disengage the head, which was covered with a greasy substance. He did so easily, but "he seemed frightened," Frith was told, "for his hands shook, and just as the Prince said, 'Look! the eye is going' (and so it was, for it turned to dust as we was looking), master's hand shook so that the head slipped through his fingers to the ground. . . . The Prince was angry, and blew master up, and told one of the gentlemen to put it back in the coffin."

The hair, according to Halford, was "of a beautiful dark brown colour. That of the beard was a redder brown. On the back part of the head it was on more than an inch in length, and had probably been cut so short for the convenience of the executioner, or perhaps by the piety of friends soon after death, in order to furnish memorials of the unhappy king." After re-sealing the coffin, the carpenter picked up a piece of the flesh of the neck and gave it to his apprentice as a keepsake, and it was this grim relic which Frith was shown when he visited the chapel in 1863. Even the elevated Halford was not immune from the lure of the souvenir, for he took part of the fourth cervical vertebra which had been severed by the axe. This he used to show at dinner parties. He relates that the coffin of Henry VIII "appeared to have been beaten in with violence about the middle; and a considerable opening in that part of it exposed a mere skeleton of the King." This fact confirmed Herbert's account in one further particular, that which concerned the impious foot-soldier.

During the very same month of 1813 in which the Prince Regent was making his investigation, another strange transaction was going forward in London. The proprietor of Bullock's Museum in Piccadilly was offered for sale the head of Oliver Cromwell. After much thought he refused it, largely owing to Lord Liverpool's objection—on aesthetic grounds—to exhibition. This was a new turn of taste, if a happy one, for many times during the course of its extra-ordinary history the head had figured as a public curiosity, first, impaled on a pole as a "warning to traitors," and later as a draw in just such museums as Bullock's. After the indignity of Tyburn, Cromwell's embalmed head was struck from his body (the nose being smashed in the process) and was borne to Westminster Hall where, with those of

Bradshaw and Ireton, it was seen by Pepys on February 6, 1661, "at the further end." There for many years it stayed. From its horrid eminence it was blown by one of two great storms, either that of May 12, 1687, or that of November 26–27, 1703. If it survived the first, it is improbable that it weathered the second, which was so violent that "London Bridge was choked up with wrecks." It was taken by the sentry at whose feet it fell. He hid it in his cloak and carried it home. Placards soon appeared requiring its return, so the sentry concealed the windfall even from his own family, stowing it in a chimney.

Before the sentry's death he revealed the find to his daughter, whose husband sold it to the Cambridgeshire family of Russell, descendants of the Protector's daughter Frances. In the course of time it descended to one Samuel Russell, an actor, who raised money by exhibiting it near Clare Market. Samuel having got into debt to one James Cox, reluctantly sold him the head in cancellation of a debt of £100, to which the sum of £18 was added. The deed of sale is dated April 30, 1787. Cox, like the sentry, was shy of showing his prize and indeed took pains to conceal it, but shortly before 1799, seeing his way to a considerable profit, he sold it to "a syndicate of three persons of democratic views" for £230. The relic was once again shown as "a revolutionary souvenir" in Mead Court, Bond Street, a visit costing half a crown. The head then passed to a single heiress, the same who offered it for sale in 1813. When the negotiations fell through, she consigned it to the care of her physician, Dr. Josiah Wilkinson, of Shortlands, Kent, by whose descendants it has been reverently preserved. Many circumstances make it likely that the head is authentic: physiognomy, even including the famous wart; the fact that it is embalmed; the broken pole stuck in the neck.

As to the whereabouts of Cromwell's body, there is great uncertainty. The most probable account relates that by special favour it was conveyed to Newburgh Priory, near Coxwold in Yorkshire, the home of his daughter Lady Fauconberg. There on the outside of a closed chamber within the house is an inscription: "In this vault are Cromwell's bones, brought here, it is believed, by his daughter Mary Countess Fauconberg at the Restoration, when his remains were disinterred from Westminster Abbey." It may be so; but whatever the truth of the matter, fate has played strange tricks with one of the greatest Englishmen. By comparison, Charles I has rested tranquilly.

8

CROMWELL IN PETTICOATS

I

ABOUT the year 1750, a certain Mr. Thomas Gardner made a discovery at Southwold. He was manager of the saltings at that sea-coast place, and, in a blacksmith's shop, he found the dies of the first medal bestowed on both officers and men of a victorious army, that for Dunbar. The blacksmith had not realized their interest, and Mr. Gardner was only able to rescue intact that for the obverse, which bore the effigy of Oliver Cromwell. From this, some specimens were struck, and it was agreed, as indeed it had been a century before, that even the incomparable Thomas Simon had never made a better likeness.

Why the dies should have been found in that particular place would have seemed a mystery until it was recalled that saltings were once worked some distance up the coast, near Yarmouth, by a certain Mrs. Bendysh, who had died a little over twenty years before. "That explains much," the local wiseacres would have remarked, for this same person was one of the most extraordinary the neighbourhood had known. Recorded gossip, and surviving specimens struck from the die, are the most tangible relics now extant of Bridget Bendysh; moreover, they are not unconnected, since she was the granddaughter of Oliver Cromwell and—if the talk is to be believed—his living image.

Cromwell ran to daughters. He loved them all, and they did him credit, more so than his sons, who were not outstanding. Bridget Bendysh was the daughter of the eldest, whose looks, as caught by Lely, reflect her father. She married his favourite officer, the redoubtable Ireton, and the lady of the saltings was the fourth of their children. She had remarkable blood, and a character to implement it. Moreover she was the daughter of the only Cromwell girl upon whom no suspicion of backsliding could ever fall, for when Ireton died his widow married Fleetwood, and did not long survive the Restoration. Elizabeth, Cromwell's favourite, predeceased him, to his sharp grief; Mary and Frances married aristocratic squires easily reconciled to the returning monarchy. Ireton's daughter was of sterner stuff. Of the many stories told of her, none is better witnessed than that which relates her recovery from a fever. She lay stricken, as some thought mortally. Her aunt, Lady Fauconberg, was with others in her sick-room, and talk turned upon the Protector. It was not flattering. Bridget lay, as all thought insensible, till she could bear no more. Suddenly, to general consternation, she raised herself up and turned upon her too complaisant aunt. "If," she said in her wrath, "if I did not believe my grandmother to have been one of the most virtuous women in the world, I should consider your ladyship a bastard. I wonder how it could be possible that the daughter of the greatest and best man that ever lived could be so degenerate as not only to sit with patience to hear his memory so ill-treated, but to seem to assent to it." Thereafter, she began to recover.

The material upon which an idea of Mrs. Bendysh may be formed was collected by the industrious Mark Noble, who wrote so much about the Cromwells in the eighteenth century, when memory of the actors in the Great Rebellion was still not too remote. "If the reader wishes to know what figure Oliver would have made in petticoats," he says, "I would recommend him to read this lady's character."

II

Bridget was born in the year of Dunbar, 1650, and from the first appears to have been a favourite of her grandfather. He discovered that she could keep a secret, an art, she said, she learnt from him. She was fond of telling that when she was only six she once sat with him at a state council meeting, and on someone objecting to her presence the Protector said: "There is no secret I would trust with any of you that I would not trust with her." To prove it, he exhorted her mother and grandmother to try with promises, bribes, caresses or threats to see whether he were not right. He never found his confidence mistaken. The attribute proved useful to her more than once later in life.

On the death of her mother, Bridget made her home with the Fleetwoods, moving in an atmosphere of active nonconformity with which she was familiar till her death. At nineteen she married a certain Mr. Thomas Bendysh of Gray's Inn and of Southtown near Great Yarmouth. They had two sons and a daughter, who make no mark in history, and not much in the life of their mother.

Bridget's interests stretched far beyond domesticities. She never lost her lively sense of public affairs, and her well-known eccentricities made a good cloak for the activities of a secret agent. Although her blood would always have made her suspect, her local reputation was so formidable that she never directly fell foul of the authorities. In that she may be accounted lucky, for she had some narrow shaves. She was quite fearless. "In particular," says one who knew her, "she delivered a relative from imprisonment for high treason, on account of the Rye House Plot, by a bold and well-conceived stratagem, though perfectly sensible that her own life must have paid the price of his escape had she been detected." The same witness adds: "If she had been in the situation of Elizabeth, she would, without scruple, have cut off the heads of twenty Marys who, by surviving her, might have overturned the happy establishment she had formed, and would as gloriously have defended her kingdom against a Spanish armada, or any hostile force whatever, and have rather inwardly triumphed, than been intimidated at the most formidable preparations against her."

The Rye House Plot, hatched in 1683, had as its design the murder of the King and the Duke of York on their way back from Newmarket, thus, it was hoped, ensuring a Protestant succession. It came to nothing; nor did Monmouth's Rebellion, for taking part in which two connections of Bridget's, the young brothers Hewling, suffered the death penalty. But she saw the Protestant cause triumph at last. She was in the secret of the Revolution of 1688, and played her modest part in the triumph of William of Orange. It is recorded that "she would go into shops in different parts of the town, under a pretext of cheapening silks and other goods, and in going out to her coach, would take the opportunity to drop bundles of papers to prepare the minds of the people for that happy event." Happy it was, for her brother Henry married the daughter of the Speaker of the new House of Commons and became a Gentleman of the Horse to King William, while later she herself had an interview with Queen Mary, to whom she was presented by Archbishop Tillotson. Had not the Queen died soon after, she might well have had a pension.

III

Bridget's appearance was so singular that it never failed to hold the attention and respect of any stranger who entered the same room, "though the company were ever so numerous, and though many of them might be more splendid." Her "highest dress" was "a plain silk, but it was usually of the richest sort, of what is called a quaker's colour; and she wore besides a kind of black silk hood, or scarf," not otherwise worn by ladies of her time. "Though hoops were in fashion long before her death, nothing could have induced her to wear one." Such was her state in company. Her daily habit was very different. "She was accustomed to turn her hands to the meanest offices and even drudgeries of life, among her workmen from the earliest morning to the decline of day; insensible to all the calls and necessities of nature, and in a habit and appearance beneath the meanest of them, and neither suiting her character nor sex; and then immediately, after having eaten and drunk almost to excess of whatever is before her, without choice or distinction, to throw herself down upon the next couch or bed that offers, in the profoundest sleep; to rise from it with new life and vigour; to dress herself in all the riches and grandeur of appearance that her present circumstances or the remains of better times allow her; and about the close of evening, to ride in her chaise, or on her pad, to a neighbouring port and there shine in conversation, and receive the place and precedence in all company, as a lady who expected at this time to have been one of the first persons in Europe."

Another witness, whom she impressed when still a child, goes still farther. "I have often seen her in the morning," he records, "stumping about with an old straw hat on her head, her hair about her ears, without stays, and when it was cold an old blanket about her shoulders and a staff in her hands—in a word, exactly accoutred to mount the stage as a witch in *Macbeth*. Yet if at such a time she were accosted by any person of rank or breeding, the dignity of her manner and politeness of style, which nothing could efface, would instantly break through."

Perhaps her greatest likeness to the Protector was the way in which she would settle her most pressing problems. "If she questions the lawfulness or expediency of any great, hazardous and doubtful undertaking, she pursues the method which she says her grandfather always employed with success; that is, she shuts herself up in her closet, till by fasting and praying the vapours are raised, and the animal spirits wrought up to an unusual ferment by an over-intenseness and strain of thinking; and whatever portion of scripture comes into her head at such a season, thence-forward no entreaties nor persuasion, no force of reason, nor plainest evidence of the same scriptures alleged against it; no conviction of the impropriety, injustice, impiety, or almost impossibility of the thing can turn her from it."

The reverse side of the medal must also be related, and indeed follows from the rest: "Of great and most fervent devotion towards God, and love to her fellow creatures, yet there is scarcely an instance of impiety or cruelty of which she is not capable. Fawning, suspicious, mistrustful, and jealous without end of all her servants and even of her friends, at the same time that she is ready to do them all the service in her power, affecting all mankind equally, and not according to the services they are able to do her, but according to the services their necessities and miseries demand from her, to the relieving of which neither the wickedness of their characters, nor the injuries they may have done herself in particular are the least exception, but rather a peculiar recommendation."

"Mrs. Bendysh," says the same witness, "was sure of the common people; she was, as she deserved to be, very dear to them; when she had money, she gave it freely to such as wanted; and when she had none, which was pretty often, they were sure of receiving civility and commiseration. She was not barely charitable, she practised an exalted humanity. If, in the meanest sick-room, she found the sufferer insufficiently or poorly attended, she turned attendant herself, and would sit hours in the poorest chamber to administer support or consolation to the afflicted."

One of her employments was the grazing of cattle. "Her

going to fairs to buy them, in the only equipage she had, a one-horse chaise, afforded exercise at once for her courage and enthusiasm; travelling in the night was the same as in the day; and in the worst roads and weathers as in the best; nor could she encounter any dangers in which it would be too little to say she was perfectly fearless; it comes nearer to her character to say, which she would not enjoy. I have heard her say that when in the darkest night, on a wild open heath, with the roads of which she was not acquainted, she has had to encounter the most dreadful thunderstorms, she has been happy, has sung this or that psalm, and doubted not that angels surrounded her chaise and protected her."

Whatever may have been the case with her own conveyance, it was sometimes different elsewhere. "Happening to travel in a London stage, in company with two gentlemen who had swords on, she informed them of her descent from Oliver, and as usual was extolling him with all that rapture to which her idolizing him to enthusiasm led her, when one of her fellow travellers descended so much below the man as to treat his memory with gross indignation and abuse. She answered it with all the spirit that was inherent in her, till the coach stopped and they got out, on which she instantly drew the other gentleman's sword, called this a poltroon and a coward, and now challenged him to shew himself a man." She had her apology in full.

IV

Among Bridget's closest friends was the great Isaac Watts, who ministered to a congregation in Mark Lane which had formerly included many eminent in the Puritan cause, Fleetwood and Disbrowe among them. Watts's own grandfather had been one of Blake's captains, perishing in the prime of life in an explosion at sea. His flock preferred him to his predecessor Chauncy, but must have sung his famous hymn, "Come let us join our cheerful song . . ." with a marked consciousness that it did indeed refer to a better world, at least until religious toleration at last became assured. Bridget knew all about persecution, when preachers "went in momentary danger of being dragged out by spies and informers to heavy fines and severe imprisonments. With these spies and informers she maintained a perpetual war. This kind of bustle was, in all respects, in the true taste of her spirit. Sometimes she circumvented and out-witted them, and sometimes she bullied them. The event generally was that she got the poor parson out of their clutches."

One disconcerting habit is recorded. She had an utter disregard of time. "As the whole of Mrs. Bendysh's personal economy was not of the common form, her hours of visiting went generally out of the common season. She would frequently come and visit a house at nine or ten at night, and sometimes later if the doors were not shut up. On such visits she generally stayed till about one in the morning. Such late visits, in these sober times, were considered by her friends as highly inconvenient, yet nobody complained of them to her. The respect she universally commanded gave her a license in this and many other irregularities. She would, on her visits, drink wine in great plenty, and the wine used to put her tongue into very brisk motion; but I do not remember," adds the narrator, "that she was ever disgracefully exposed by it."

And so she drives away into the darkness, careless of wind and rain, singing one of the psalms so beloved of her grandfather, conveying into the sober reign of George I something of the rough zest of a more heroic time. With her perished the last savour of Old Noll.

9

SIR RICHARD STAYNER

I

WHILE the fighting seaman of to-day must be awake to perils above and beneath the face of the waters as well as upon them, he is spared three evils known all too well to his forebears. The marine engine and the wireless telegraph have between them eased the threat of storm; radar has simplified navigation unrecognizably; while the ill-health referred to again and again in the biographies of past generations is less heard of, since improvement in conditions of service and in the building of ships has been vast.

Many men have worn themselves out keeping open the sea-ways, the immortal Blake and some of the best of his captains among them. Of this band, Richard Stayner, who lived and died at sea, has an eminent place. Stayner made his final return to Spithead in November 1662, in His Majesty's ship the *Mary*, after a voyage from Lisbon. That pleasing Garrison Church, which had seen the marriage of Charles II and Catherine of Braganza in May of the same year, witnessed his final home-coming. His embalmed body, by his express wish, was to lie near that of his wife, who had died in the time of Old Noll.

The event was not much remarked by the world at large, yet within a day of the ship's arrival a man in London duly noted the fact, as was his way. "This morning," wrote Pepys, "we had news by letters that Sir Richard Stayner is dead, which we are sorry for, he being a very stout seaman." Pepys knew him of old, and himself attended the last obsequies of one whose whole life was spent on active service, generally afloat, often abroad, and never in great commands. He left neither a memorable portrait behind him nor any sort of memorialist, and his name, therefore, is seldom recalled; but he was in fact, what Pepys's few words indicate, one of those quiet and resolute officers upon whom, then as since, England's safety has depended. He has, moreover, another claim to attention; for it so chanced that it was from spoils of his winning that some of the finest coins in the whole English series were minted. His name, indeed, links with Blake and Monck at sea, with Simon and Blondeau in the realm of numismatics, while he had the distinction (shared with Dick Ingoldsby) of being knighted both by Cromwell and by Charles II.

The historian rightly laments that too little detail is known of Blake's early life, though at last, after nearly three centuries, he has an honourable memorial in Westminster Abbey. With Stayner, as with so many of his sea contemporaries, the gaps are still wider; though once fairly launched as a commander of State's ships, his career is not hard to follow. He first appears towards middle life, when he had charge of the *Elizabeth*, a small vessel carrying two sakers—guns equivalent to six-pounders. The *Elizabeth* was fitted out "for surprising small pickaroons that lurk among the sands" of the Essex coast, and for convoy service in the North Sea. In August 1649 he had his first recorded success. He captured a small frigate, the *Robert*, one of a force under Prince Rupert. For this and other good work he was given twenty pounds, with a further five pounds for a gold medal. Henceforward he was a favoured man. Three years later he was in command of the *Mermaid*, fitting out at Chatham, and by January 1653 had exchanged to the *Foresight*, in which ship he took part in the Battle of Portland, where he bore himself with distinction, and at the Gabbard. He was with the White Squadron under Penn in that stiff fight with Tromp, and it was from this ship that, with many of his colleagues, he signed the Declaration made on the Dissolution of Parliament by Cromwell. They aimed "not to meddle with State affairs, but to keep foreigners from fooling us."

After the Gabbard the *Foresight* was sent into the Thames to escort twelve disabled ships, eleven Dutch prizes, 1,350 prisoners, and to convey the body of Admiral Deane to Woolwich. Stayner returned to the fleet in time to take part in the fight of July 29th to 31st. He then found himself under the orders of Monck, who, always ready to advance an efficient captain, sponsored his appeal for a larger ship. In January 1654 he was appointed to the *Plymouth*, of more than 900 tons, and a ship that was later to take part in his biggest independent action. In her he made a cruise in the North Sea, taking prizes, including one Dutch East Indiaman of 800 tons which had on board four chests of silver.

In July he transferred to the *Catherine*, and in September sailed with Blake for the Mediterranean. This expedition, Blake's second, and an early instance of the many when a great commander made the English flag respected in that vital sea, took a year. Stayner returned home with his Admiral in the autumn of 1655. Blake, who had every reason to know his value, again took him with him early in the year following, this time in the *Bridgewater*. They sailed to Cadiz, which was then under close blockade.

Here was to be the scene of Stayner's one personal triumph. In September 1656 Blake and Montagu left him off the port in command of six or seven ships, his flag being in the *Speaker*. It was the English hope that they would intercept a Spanish treasure fleet coming in from the west. On the 8th, Spaniards were sighted. At first they thought Stayner's squadron to be fishing craft, although the *Speaker*, with the *Plymouth* and the *Bridgewater* which were in company, were all sizeable vessels. They had been deceived by information given by a prize, which had seen the rest of the fleet on its way to Aveiro. The mistake was further excusable in view of the weather, which was bad when the forces first made contact. Stayner reported: "At night it blew so hard westerly, by means whereof we with our squadron weighed out of the bay at Cadiz, and plied to sea. In the evening we espied eight sail. . . ." Next day, the 9th, the Spanish were made out to be a fleet from Havana, King's ships, merchant-men, and a Portuguese prize. They were laden with gold, silver, pearls, indigo, sugar, spices, and tobacco. The place, the foe, and the opportunity were all such as to recall great occasions in the days of Elizabeth.

It was not in the nature of Cromwell's admirals to be less adventurous. Although in the darkness of the night the Spanish admiral had vanished with his prize, and others had driven far to leeward, Stayner brought his three biggest ships into close action. Their sailing and fighting qualities were all well known to him. They had, in his own words, "hot dispute" with four capital ships. Three struck; the fourth escaped towards Cadiz, hit a rock, and foundered. Some of the smaller vessels were snapped up later.

The victory was complete, the immediate harvest less so; for of the captured ships two caught fire, being lost with all their cargo and most of their men, including the Vice-Admiral. Of his one floating prize Stayner first reported: "The captain of her, which we have on board, saith she hath in her two millions of silver." This proved to be an over-estimate, though the total Spanish loss exceeded that large sum. Stayner actually secured much treasure, and added a new glory to his commander's fame.

There followed jubilation. The national prestige, furthered by strength in arms, had seldom stood higher on the Continent, which was then as now impressed by success, even at the hands of a government frowned upon by the Dynasties. In October a General Thanksgiving was held in London, and an official narrative of the battle appeared.

In November the fleet arrived at Portsmouth with the prizes. Major-General Thomas Kelsey, one of the Commissioners of the Admiralty, went down to see the bullion safely conveyed to London. It was carried in thirty-eight wagons, loaded with ingots of "sugar-loaf" silver, "pina" silver, cakes and bars of silver, wrought plate, and, in Peruvian coin, pieces of 8 and pieces of $\frac{1}{2}$. The silver was contained in fifty-six chests, the total weight being 14,221 lb. 8 oz. 1 dwt. Thurloe, Cromwell's secretary, says that the amount originally taken was nearly a million pounds, but that "all was plundered down to about £350,000 or £300,000 sterling." He also mentions cups and flagons, boxes of chocolate and drugs, bags of wool, an inlaid bedstead, and some fine tortoise-shell.

That was indeed no trifle. Parliament ordered that a large part should be melted, assayed, and used in the Tower Mint, and that two thousand pounds should be set apart for new coinage designed by the peerless Thomas Simon and manufactured with that new machinery which Peter Blondeau, in the face of every form of obstruction from the established coiners, was trying to introduce. The resultant series of coins (some with legends in the common tongue for the first and last time, and the best bearing the effigy of Cromwell) are at once the triumph of a great artist, and a still tangible relic of a notable victory at sea. This money, diverted in fair fight from the coffers of the King of Spain, is still prized among collectors, as it was from the start. Here Pepys— never more astute than over objects of vertu—is again in point. He was a warm admirer of Blondeau's improvements, and so, after the Restoration, was Slingsby, Master of the Mint. Dining with Pepys some years after Charles had returned, Slingsby had a surprise for his host. He produced "the new pieces both of gold and silver (examples of them all) that were made for the King by Blondeau's way; and compared them with those made for Oliver. The pictures of the latter made by Simon, and of the King by one Rotyr

82

(*i.e.* John Roettiers), a German, I think, that dined with us also . . . but upon my word, those of the Protector are more like, in my mind, than the King's. . . . The crownes of Cromwell are now sold, it seems, for 25s. and 30s. apiece." Never since have they declined in interest or value.

II

Stayner rejoined Blake early in 1657, and in April of that year shared in a last engagement under his command. It was that against the Spanish West India fleet at Santa Cruz. On this occasion his valour was outstanding, his leadership no less so, and for his part in the victory he was knighted by the Protector. This action was Blake's last. He died of fever on his way home to England. Clarendon said of Santa Cruz: "The whole action was so miraculous that all men who knew the place wondered any sober man, with what courage soever endowed, would ever have undertaken it." Such was no unworthy praise from a royalist. To Stayner had fallen the honour of beginning the assault.

With the passing of Blake, Stayner's career was less adventurous, though he still prospered in his chosen profession. He was in command in the Downs in 1658, nominally second to Montagu, who was, however, mostly away in London. He flew his flag as Rear-Admiral in the *Essex*, the *London*, or his own famous *Speaker*. He remained at his post when Cromwell died, and during the perplexed period of the Interregnum, while his old commander, Monck, was playing his astute part in bringing about a peaceful Restoration. Nor was he deprived of his rank when the great changes in government took place. Montagu appointed him Rear-Admiral of the fleet which brought the King to his own again. He was in close attendance when the sovereign embarked, and was knighted anew by Charles. Pepys met him in those halcyon days. "Sir R. Stayner," he records on

May 3, 1660, "who had invited us yesterday, took all the Commanders and myself on board him to dinner."

Even in the turmoil of the early Restoration there was room enough towards the top for men eminent in their profession. Experienced naval officers were cherished if their political opinions were not of too glaring a hue, and neither Charles nor his brother James nor Admiral Montagu was disposed to displace Stayner. In the summer of 1661 he was ordered from the Downs to Lisbon and the Mediterranean, once more as Rear-Admiral under Montagu, now Earl of Sandwich, patron and friend of Pepys.

Sandwich returned in 1662, leaving Stayner, flying his flag in the *Mary*, as Rear-Admiral under Sir John Lawson. He did not long survive the change of command. In July he was reported to be ill at Lisbon. He died there on October 9th, worn out by the rigours of a long life at sea. The *Mary*, the ship which bore his body home, was indeed fitted to do so, for she was formerly the *Speaker*, his flagship at Cadiz. He had been present when the King re-named her.

The details of Stayner's career which have come down to us are mainly comprised in a handful of letters and reports from active service addressed to the Commonwealth Generals of the fleet. He was the type of commander in which the maritime history of this country is rich; men who have helped to build up that "combat supremacy" upon which Mahan insisted so forcibly as being one of the pillars of seapower.

Of lowly Dorset blood, he died wealthy, investing in—among other properties—the "Catherine Wheel" at Greenwich. A son predeceased him; his daughter married a Gloucestershire land-owner and brought as part of her dowry a splendid pearl and emerald necklace, taken by her father as spoil of Cadiz.

IO

THE GREAT LORD HAWKE

I

ALTHOUGH the national memory has a way of keeping green many great events, in this respect it is capricious. It is the same with great men. Here idiosyncrasy and mere chance play their part. Admiral Benbow, for instance, is known, like Admiral Vernon, from many inn signs; but a closer examination of the careers of either men, while it throws light on the reason why they so caught the popular imagination, also shows a measure of this caprice. Vernon is remembered chiefly for his introduction of grog, and Benbow for a fine name, a martial aspect, and a fighting end. Yet neither men, in point of professional skill, can compare with the victor of Quiberon Bay.

As if to do something to redress the balance, two old songs are still sung, one closely and the other remotely linked with Hawke's career. The first is *Heart of Oak*, with music by Boyce, which made its début in Garrick's pantomime *Harlequin's Invasion*, produced to celebrate the passing of the danger from which Hawke had delivered his country. Familiar though they are, the words are worth study as an instance of how, sometimes in minute particulars, the same incidents, threats, and dangers recur. The second is Cowper's *Toll for the Brave*, which commemorates the loss of the *Royal George* in 1782. She had carried Hawke to triumph nearly a quarter of a century before.

II

When George Monck, who knew something of the art of war, wished to describe the principal virtues needed, he

85

used the words, "valour and sufferance." Of the two, "sufferance," or patient endurance, with the mind on a single purpose, is usually accounted the harder to achieve. It has always been the cardinal element in the exercise of sea-power, whose relentless pressure, slow and silent, has inevitably been the core of any success, offensive and defensive, which this country has known.

In the career of Edward Hawke is seen every element of the great professional sea-officer. His rise was slow though certain, marked by occasional brilliance, helped little by the favour of politicians. It culminated, after years of patience and sometimes of bitter disappointment, in an opportunity such as comes but once in a lifetime, and then not to every commander; one which demanded each scrap of that skill and knowledge which had accumulated over the years. Although Quiberon Bay, St. Vincent, and Trafalgar were won by brilliance in the heat of battle, they would all have been impossible without that "sufferance," understanding, co-ordination, and planning which must be built up slowly, and with the utmost care, by a commander and his principal subordinates. "May our officers have the eye of a Hawke," was an old naval toast. It is worth recalling how that eye was trained.

Hawke's father was Cornish, but he married a grand-daughter of Sir William Fairfax of Steeton, and he was thus connected with the Yorkshire family which gave the Commonwealth eminent leaders. It was to the mother's family, the Bladens, that the son looked for what advancement might come his way independent of his own merit. This was not much, for it was the older Pitt who ruled in Westminster in Hawke's heyday and Pitt's coldness was consistent. One piece of good fortune he did enjoy was the favour of his sovereign. George II had a better nose for a fighter than some of his ministers, which was not surprising since he had led troops in person in the field of battle. He prevented

Hawke from being shelved at a moment critical in his career.

Hawke had been twenty-four years at sea, serving in many parts of the world, and with his country more often than not at war, before he saw action. He was by that time almost forty, and was in command of the *Berwick*, of seventy guns, at the battle of Toulon. He had a reputation in the service of being an efficient officer, but ill-starred, and the course of this engagement did nothing to alter the general view. His ship was handled with great skill in a poorly conducted operation. She beat the Spanish *Neptune* out of the line, while the *Poder* too should have been her prize, but of this she was robbed by the misconduct of an officer, who allowed her to be burnt.

Three years after this battle there was a wholesale promotion of captains, made chiefly in order to elevate Boscawen. Hawke would then have been retired but for the King's emphatic ruling that "he would not have him yellowed." George had had his eye on him ever since he read the Toulon despatches. The result was fortunate, for during the next thirty years Hawke, despite indifferent health, was in positions of high responsibility almost throughout, to the great benefit of the fleet. He flew his flag in the Channel command, the Western fleet, the Mediterranean, and ended his long career in the highest post to which a naval officer could aspire—as First Lord of the Admiralty. He was no unworthy successor to Anson, and he had the knowledge of a magnificent band of officers risen and rising, eager to carry on his work, one which included Howe, the Hoods, and Rodney, some of whom had served under him in action, and of whom all had benefited by his example.

Although professionally Hawke received little check, and came to be regarded as indispensable, fortune was still not wholly kind. While maintaining the great blockade of the French—Brest in his day was a sealed port from May to

November—he missed decisive engagements at one time or another with De la Motte, la Gallissonniere, and Bompart—glittering names in French naval history. He had, moreover, the disappointment of seeing the failure of a combined operation off Rochefort in 1757. The youthful Wolfe was one of the soldiers who chafed at inaction in that affair, and was so soon to prove how much better he could himself do in circumstances of greater difficulty. No blame attached to Hawke, who had brought the troops to the right place without molestation, and could scarcely be held responsible for the weather, or the hesitancy of the generals.

When Hawke had been knighted, in 1747, he adopted a motto of characteristic pith—the single word "Strike." The honour was bestowed for his successful action against the heavy escort of a French convoy from Rochelle, bound for America. The convoy itself escaped annihilation, though by sending word to the West Indies he ensured the ultimate destruction of the greater part. The action showed two things clearly. The first was that Hawke (unlike Rodney on some occasions) would always prefer to keep his force cohesive rather than disperse it in pursuit of prizes. The second was that he did not expect his captains to adhere like robots to the Admiralty "Fighting Instructions" of the day. "For God's sake," he wrote later in life to his friend Geary, "if you should be so lucky as to get sight of the enemy, get as close to them as possible. Do not let them shuffle with you by engaging at a distance, but get within musket-shot if you can; that will be the way to gain great honour, and will be the means to make the action decisive." A few decades later, Nelson was acting on that precept.

III

The comparison between our own days and those of the Napoleonic wars is often pressed. In some ways a still more instructive parallel lies in the time when the seeds were sown of Britain's maritime and Colonial supremacy—the years of the Austrian Succession and Seven Years War. Here Hawke's victory at Quiberon Bay stands in the precise relationship that Trafalgar did to the struggle with Napoleon. It was decisive, and it took place, like Trafalgar, some years before the closing of the struggle.

The Seven Years War, and Wolfe, gave us Canada, but we paid a price which is yet being paid, for the conflict not only determined Britain's future overseas, it foreshadowed that in the Prussia of Frederick the Great was to lie the dreadful future of Germany. Frederick opposed Austria for German supremacy, and won, though the victory took time to mature. Austria's policy, in the interest of her non-German possessions—Hungary and the Italian provinces—was to keep Germany weak. France took her side.

France has known many vicissitudes since, as has Germany; but when Hitler declared that the Reich was at last organized on a Frederickian model, he was merely stating that the fruits of the Seven Years War had come to their ripening. Although we fought in 1758 as Frederick's allies, he complained bitterly that we were conducting one sort of war and he another, and that we were little use to him. Frederick indeed helped much in the creation of the European legend of perfidious Albion. But in a sense he was right. Britain was discovering one way of development, Prussia another, and in the long run, they were utterly antagonistic. The Continental enemy might differ from era to era; the principle remained—that a tolerable balance of power in Europe was essential to the peace of the western hemisphere, and to Britain's trading interests. Whenever it has been forgotten, it has meant danger, and generally war.

It is too much to claim for Quiberon Bay that it affected the European balance of power in anything but a temporary way. What can be said with truth is that it was one of the most decisive sea battles since the Armada, and that it was the first of a series of victories which, from that day to this, have given the Royal Navy predominance in European waters.

The immediate circumstances of the action were as follows: the French had an army assembled in the Morbihan in Brittany for the invasion of these shores. Flat-bottomed boats were ready for that dash across the Channel so often planned, and so often thwarted by those storm-tossed ships and their commanders on whom the safety of our realm principally depends. Dunkirk, Havre, Brest, L'Orient, these, as so lately, were names heard on every lip.

The French movement overseas was to be covered by a fleet made up by uniting the Toulon and Brest squadrons. Boscawen smashed the Toulon force, but that in Brest remained, and the troops were still encamped. Choiseul, the French minister, thought that Conflans at Brest should meet the British at sea before attempting to cover the military expedition. If the encounter were disastrous, the troops would not be lost; if otherwise, the way would be clear.

About November 5, 1759, a tremendous gale blew from the west. Hawke, who had already kept his fleet at sea longer than the timid considered prudent, bore up from his station off Brest and ran into Torbay, where he waited for the wind to shift. In his absence, Bompart's force from the West Indies slipped in to join Conflans. His seasoned crews were distributed among the waiting ships, and Conflans, finding an easterly wind on the 14th, put to sea, and stood at once to southward, believing he had eluded Hawke.

But the wind blew for friend and foe alike. Hawke, who had again sailed out from Torbay on the 12th, had been driven back. He issued a third time on the same day as Conflans. Reaching his accustomed position, he soon had news of the direction in which the enemy had been seen. He guessed they were bound for Quiberon Bay. Thither he shaped his own course, under press of sail, and as his great ships rolled on their way, the London mob was burning him in effigy for not having already brought his foes to account.

On the 19th, Conflans saw ships ahead of him, and thought them to be those of Commodore Duff, who was blockading Quiberon. He was right. Conflans gave the order to chase. Duff's squadron then divided. One division went before the wind, the other hauled up to southward. Conflan's main force followed Duff's first division, that is, it held towards the coast. It was not long after this that the French rear signalled ships to windward. Hawke's moment had come. On the morning of November 20th the frigate *Maidstone*, ahead of the English fleet, sighted the enemy.

The French could not at first credit Hawke's diligence, and that his principal force could be at hand. Conflans ordered his rear division to haul to wind and chase Duff's second group, of which only one French ship was then in pursuit. A few minutes later, and it was seen that Hawke's fleet now coming up was of twenty-three ships, including three-deckers. Conflans had twenty-one. Caught as he was, his position, according to the precedents of naval warfare, seemed anything but desperate. It was now blowing hard from the west-north-west, with every appearance of heavy weather, and the ships were on a lee shore. Conflans had merely to lead in among the rocks and shoals of Quiberon Bay, and he should be safe. He did so.

Hawke, who had waited so long for this moment, did not hesitate. "There was a demon in him that wild winter day," says Corbett, "that knew no rule nor risk." He hurled his ships pell-mell after the French, making their movements serve for his own navigation, following hard in their wake. "Form as you chase," was his order. The guns roared out against the thunder of the surf. As Conflans rounded the Cardinals, the venomous rocks at the entrance to Quiberon Bay, the broadsides of the leading English ships were brought to bear on the French rear. Hawke, breaking all convention, was fighting an action in a scene of Handelian grandeur in a way for which there was no precedent. No one but a seaman experienced to the marrow, would have thought to snatch victory under the very cliffs of a hostile shore.

Waiting was over, and glory before his eyes. The first French ship to be engaged, finding herself pressed and out-manoeuvred, opened her lower-deck ports. The sea swept in, and she sank with most of her company. The *Royal George* herself took another. Then another struck, flying a com-modore's pennant; a fourth sunk, and the rest were scattered. Seven fled to the mouth of the little river Vilaine, into which they entered at the top of the tide, jettisoning their guns and stores as they did so. This was a feat never done before, and by it four were lost to the French navy, for they broke their backs. Others fled south to Rochefort, one being wrecked near the mouth of the Loire. The flagship, *Soleil Royal*, rode out in the night off Croisie. Next day, when Conflans found himself alone, he ran his ship ashore near Croisie to keep her out of English hands.

"Night was now come," wrote Hawke, "and being on a part of the coast among islands and shoals, of which we were totally ignorant, without a pilot, as was the greatest part of the Squadron, and blowing hard on a lee shore, I made the signal to anchor." Not all his ships heard the signal guns from the *Royal George*, and the night was made terrible by unknown distress. Two English ships were gone by morning, the *Essex* and the *Resolution*. They ran upon a shoal, but most of their men were saved, and the wrecks were burnt. Hawke lost altogether about fifty men, once again showing how victory may come almost bloodlessly to the skilled commander.

"When I consider the season of the year," he said in his despatch, "the hard gales on the day of action, a flying enemy, the shortness of the day, and the coast they were on, I can boldly affirm that all that could possibly be done has been done. Had we had but two hours more daylight, the whole had been totally destroyed or taken; for we were almost up with their van when night overtook us."

So much may be done in one short day, if there is a Hawke on board the flagship, and if he leads Englishmen. Ten thousand people on the shore had seen their might humbled by sea-power.

Of the many factors which contributed to Hawke's achievement, one of the most decisive, apart from his tactical courage, was his care of the fleet itself. While he lived, this was a standing blessing. For at least forty years after his passing there was never so effective a blockade, kept up until so late in the year, and the reason was that never before had a fleet been so well cared for and supplied. Hawke organized an adequate system of shore-relief for his men, he did his best to feed them adequately, not always with success, and although, like every other officer of his day, he complained of the quality of the seamen supplied, he turned them quickly enough into first-rate fighting material.

If the effects of the battle were weighty, the immediate rewards were less so. The Bay of Biscay might be an English sea for the rest of the war, Quiberon Bay and the Basque Roads fleet anchorages, their islands cabbage-patches for the seaman's refreshment, but the men soon complained of the home authorities that

> Now Mountseer's beat
> We've nought to eat
> Since you have nought to fear.

Although Hawke himself wrote on December 16, 1759, that he had already been thirty-one weeks on board, he was not ashore in England until another full month was out. He arrived in London on January 21, 1760, and was most flatteringly received at court. But Pitt and Anson were less handsome. Hawke benefited little from Pitt's term of office, though he was found indispensable by the great war minister. As for Anson, it detracts little from the reputation of a great man to believe him somewhat jealous of Hawke's triumph. He himself had been made a peer for less. Hawke waited until he was seventy-one before he attained the eminence of the House of Lords.

Of the rest of Hawke's life, it is true to say that it was solely devoted to the interests of the naval service. What little is known of his private life is happy. His friendships were firm and many, his character that of a man devoted to a single end, the glory of his country, and the good of his men. His care for them has been indicated, as has his cardinal principle of successful action—the necessity for concentration upon one main object, the destruction of the enemy. When he died in 1781 his influence over his sea contemporaries was so paramount that, although there was brilliance in plenty soon to show itself, Horace Walpole could write: "Lord Hawke is dead, and does not seem to have bequeathed his mantle to anybody." His monument at North Stoneham in Hampshire records, without exaggeration, that "wherever he sailed victory attended him."

I I

BRAVE KEMPENFELT

I

By the accident of a lady asking Cowper for words to set to Handel's march in *Scipio*, Admiral Kempenfelt, with the eight hundred or so who perished with him in the *Royal George*, has gone down to history principally as the victim of one of the more sensational mishaps in the annals of the navy. Cowper's song, *Toll for the Brave*, is memorable enough, though somewhat inaccurate, and in stating that the Admiral's "fingers held the pen" when he sank, he conveyed the fact that Kempenfelt and literature were pretty well acquainted.

Kempenfelt's father was a Swede who spent a lifetime in the British service, under James II and Anne. He died as Lieutenant-Governor of Jersey in George I's time. We perhaps know something of his character through the accident of his being a friend of Dick Steele. They both entered the army as volunteers, served as young officers in the Guards, then their ways parted. Magnus Kempenfelt got a company in the 4th Foot, and later became a colonel; Steele, leading a very different life, wrote some of the best pages of the *Spectator* and created, in the club or society of which he described Sir Roger de Coverley as the fisrt member, a group with whom we are almost as familiar as with Chaucer's Pilgrims or the figures in Boswell. Of this club the fourth member was Captain Sentry, Sir Roger's nephew and heir, "a Gentleman of great Courage, good Understanding, but invincible Modesty." He is lightly sketched in both by Steele and Addison, and in the *Spectator* for November 24, 1742, Steele winds him up. He makes

Sentry say that he is to keep a table at Coverley for officers of slender purses but deserving parts, also "horses, servants, and all things necessary for their accommodation and enjoyment of life in a pleasant and various country." "No man," he adds, "could be more welcome than Colonel *Campenfeld*." This is an ingenious and pleasant way of drawing a character and then putting a reader off the scent.

Having a father blessed with Steele's acquaintance and, if Sentry be any guide, a gift of silence, young Richard Kempenfelt grew up with a predilection for verse. He must have inherited remarkable powers of self-suppression; for not until he was fifty-nine did he publish a collection of *Original Poems and Hymns*, and even then it was issued quietly at Exeter under the pseudonym "Philotheorus." Moreover, there were in all only nine compositions. They were dedicated to Fletcher of Madeley, and were described as "Juvenile Attempts at Sacred Poesy," although one poem at least is recorded as having been written near Sicily in 1769, when the author was middle-aged. They show fervent religious enthusiasm, and the first, which is called *The Alarm*, is a bizarre and typically eighteenth-century conjuration of Doomsday:

> Horrors invest the skies;
> Graves burst, and myriads rise;
> Nature in agonies
> Yields up her store.

All are perfectly in keeping with the outlook of the time.

Ink may be said, therefore, to have followed Kempenfelt from cradle to sea-bed, since in addition to the illustrious Cowper a multitude of lesser scribes made the most of the disaster to the *Royal George*.

Until near the end of his life Kempenfelt's career was much the same as had been his father's: steady, honourable, his rise the result of merit, not of favour. He was born in

QUIBERON BAY

The fleets encounter. From a painting by Serres in the National Maritime Museum, Greenwich

1718, joined the navy as a youth, and first saw action at the taking of Portobello. In 1741 he was lieutenant in the *Strafford*, wearing Vernon's flag, and for the next forty years, until his own promotion to Admiral's rank, was seldom independently employed. His first command was the *Lightning* fireship, but a year later, in 1757, he was transferred to the *Elizabeth*, where flew the broad pendant of Steevens. With Steevens he sailed to the East Indies, serving with him in the *Grafton* and the *Norfolk*, being present at the reduction of Pondicherry. These were the great days of Clive in India; and although the part played by sea-power was not sensational it was as essential as ever.

Steevens died in the East, but Kempenfelt remained as flag-captain to his successor Cornish. He was at the taking of Manila, and served for a time as Governor of Cavite before being sent home with despatches. He then returned to the East Indies, bringing the *Norfolk* back in 1764. He called her, years later, a "remarkable fine ship."

There followed a period of more leisure. The Peace of Paris admitted much-needed relief in that relentless struggle with France and Spain, which seems in retrospect to span the better part of the eighteenth century. Kempenfelt took the chance, the first in his life, to travel on the Continent. The Sicilian poem shows that he spent some of those years in Mediterranean waters, having time for once for that contemplation to which he was inclined.

> Straight let my wand'ring soul with rapture gaze,
> And read thy works, O Nature, with amaze;
> Cast off awhile the load of earthly cares,
> And view the Eternal in yon round of stars. . . .

Much of these years was spent in France, and far otherwise than in dreaming. Their exact course is unknown; their fruits, however, greatly benefited the navy. They are seen first in Kempenfelt's correspondence with Barham, then Comptroller, and later, after many set-backs and trials, in a

G

complete revolution in fleet signalling, which had been ripe for overhaul at least since the days of Anne. The zealous captain had taken advantage of a priceless opportunity to study the technical methods of the enemy.

Kempenfelt had returned from the East with a first-class reputation in his own service, though he was little known to the public. This was the result of experience, study, and a scientific mind. His relations with Howe and Barham show him resolute in his attempt to get the best Continental theories of naval warfare understood and adopted by his contemporaries. He made a special study of the work of de Morogues, writer of a classic treatise on Naval Tactics; of de la Bourdonnais, of whom he writes, "Signals should be simple, clear, and easily discernible. I don't know any more perfect than those invented by M. de la Bourdonnais;" and of Bourdé de Villehuet. He translated the whole of Villehuet's chapter on "Signals" for Barham's benefit. Nor was his perseverance wasted. In the years to come the lessons of the leaders of French thought were learnt, or at least used to far clearer advantage by their foes than by their own compatriots.

Put briefly, the purpose which lay behind Kempenfelt's endeavour was first to organize the fleet efficiently, and then, by issuing a comprehensive code of signals ("Instructions Explanatory to the Signal Book"), to free Admirals from the trammels of "Fighting Instructions," enabling them to make signals appropriate to any given situation or emergency, and to have them clearly understood. "Our enemies have theory," he wrote; "we are superior in practice." It was his aim that his own service should be pre-eminent in both. He did not live to see the full ripening of his ideas; while he served he was under necessity of subordinating some of his pet reforms to others, less good as he thought, evolved by Howe ("he being a popular character"), but he never made the error of being too far ahead of even the advanced opinion of his time, and immediately after his death Howe put the cream of his thought to the proof in what Corbett calls the "unrivalled tactical feat" of relieving Gibraltar in the face of the Spanish fleet. Nelson's victories, too, owe something to Kempenfelt. They came at a time when reforms were coming to full acceptance. It was Nelson's "band of brothers," his captains, who were the prime instruments of his success; but never again was it possible, once the new code of signals was in proper use and Kempenfelt's tactical grouping of ships understood, for such incomplete victories and such considerable misinterpretations of a commander's intentions as had occurred under, for instance, Rodney.

In 1770 Kempenfelt was back in active command, being appointed to the *Buckingham*. Eight years later, by that time a very senior captain, he was given the *Alexander*—ninety-four guns. He next served as Captain of the Fleet or "First Captain" successively to old Sir Charles Hardy, to Hawke's friend Geary, and to Vice-Admiral George Darby. It was a difficult post, even with better flag officers. These were all poor appointments, the outcome of Sandwich's disagreement with Keppel. "I don't suppose," said Kempenfelt, "there is an officer in the whole State whose duty is so vague and undetermined as that of an Admiral's First Captain." His trials are well illustrated by a story usually told of the year 1779. One day, when exercising the ships with the new signals, a fleet, supposed to be that of the enemy, hove in sight. The Admiral, Geary, grew restive. Going up to Kempenfelt, and laying his hand gently on his shoulder, he exclaimed with good-natured earnestness, "Now, my dear Kempy, do for God's sake, my dear Kempy, oblige me by throwing your signals overboard and make that which we all understand: 'Bring the enemy to close action!' "

It is fair to add that clearer heads than Geary's at first misliked the new system. Durham, later Kempenfelt's flag-lieutenant, has a story of how even Jervis and Duncan, men famed in later naval history, came to Kempy to protest they could not follow the new signals. "The old Admiral," says Durham, "was affected even to tears, and requested them to try them for that cruise." They were converted.

In 1780 came Kempenfelt's own promotion to Rear-Admiral of the Blue. This delighted the fleet. Sandwich, then First Lord, was indeed right when he wrote in the year following, "No officer has given more satisfaction to the nation than yourself; they have a confidence in you which could not easily be transferred to another person."

England, having allowed herself to drift into the unpopular war with her American colonies, also faced trouble in India, Gibraltar, Ireland, and Holland. Once more she was at grips with the French and Spanish at sea. 1781 was a poor year in the national fortunes, one of the poorest. Most of Northern Europe was leagued in the Armed Neutrality, an association formed to try to counter the effects of the British blockade. The French under de Grasse entered the Chesapeake, an episode which has never been forgotten in America, and an act of friendship which has since been repaid a thousandfold by American sympathy and help to France. There was an indecisive battle at the Dogger Bank between the English and the Dutch, reminiscent of the days of Blake and Tromp. Then, to crown the sad year, came the surrender at Yorktown.

Yet there was one gleam. Kempenfelt, in his first and only important command, obtained a triumph, not the less welcome for being unexpected. He was no longer a young man, and all his training and experience, though tending to produce a first-rate staff officer, might not have shown to advantage in swift decision, in seizing the brief opportunities of an action at sea. Yet the course of events was as follows.

It was winter, December. Kempenfelt, with twelve ships of the line and some frigates, was ordered to intercept a large French convoy bound for the West Indies. His information was that he was unlikely to encounter more than seven French men-of-war as escort, which would give him a decisive margin of strength. Admiralty intelligence was faulty. On December 12th, while fifty leagues to the southwest of Ushant, Kempenfelt came upon his quarry, but found the covering force to consist of nineteen ships, under the redoubtable de Guichen. With him were the Marquis de Vaudreuil, La Motte-Picquet, D'Entrecasteaux, and two other flag officers. The aggregate of guns was 1,582 as against Kempenfelt's 996.

De Guichen at once formed his line between Kempenfelt and the convoy, anticipating that the British would attack him. His dispositions may have been theoretically correct, but he had committed a major error upon which Kempenfelt seized in a flash. De Guichen, it is true, was between the English and the convoy, but he was to leeward of his charges. Kempenfelt passed astern of the French line under a press of sail, got to windward of the merchantmen, then swung his ships in among them. De Guichen was powerless. Kempenfelt captured fifteen supply ships, sank two or three more, and dispersed the rest, of which most returned to Brest. Five of these were picked up later. It was a neat and brilliant feat of arms, of which Spithead and Plymouth saw the trophies. The whole war saw no more perfect small action. It was fought on a wild and misty day, and had two far-reaching results. De Guichen resigned his command; and Rodney, knowing the West Indian supplies to be destroyed, was able to sail with full confidence of success to his last great command and to the victory of "The Saints" against de Grasse.

Kempenfelt had flown his flag in the *Victory*, Nelson's *Victory*, then in her seventeenth year. But for Trafalgar, it was her proudest engagement. "If he had done so much with so little," wrote Laughton of this fight, "what might Kempenfelt not have done had he been properly supported?"

Kempenfelt, always popular, became for a short time a hero, although the King wrote a pettish letter complaining that he had not done more. The following year he transferred his flag to the *Royal George*, being second-in-command to Admiral Barrington, his duty to watch Brest. He served in the summer cruise under Lord Howe, and on August 15, 1782, the *Royal George* anchored with the rest of the fleet at Spithead. She was to form part of the force detailed for the relief of Gibraltar.

In order to remedy an unimportant defect below the water-line it was necessary to heel the ship. There was more than one way by which this could have been done. That chosen was to shift the heavy gear, including the guns. The operation proved too much for the worn structure. With a great crack part of the bottom gave way, and the ship sank swiftly, taking a store-lighter with her and the greater part of her company, including many civilians from Portsmouth. Such is the version of those who gave evidence at the court martial, though the story popularized by Cowper of her being "overset" is more widely believed.

It is improbable that the finding of the court erred. It was composed of thirteen distinguished officers, including Barrington, Milbanke, Alexander, Hood, Hotham, Jervis, and Duncan. The ship sank on August 29th; the Court sat on September 9th, and acquitted the Captain, Martin Waghorn, who had survived. The verdict was that "the ship was not overheeled," but "that some material part of her frame gave way, which can only be accounted for by the general state of decay of her timbers." Attempts were made later to raise her, but no tears were shed in the Navy Office when these failed. An unpleasant story of official obstruction surrounds the whole circumstances of the sinking; ironically enough, it was Kempenfelt himself who wrote in 1779 to Barham: "More docks are required for repairing ships. In peace, many ships that want repairs, and which might be done at no great expense if taken in hand, soon become repairless . . . for when a ship's frame begins to decay, if the defective parts are not soon removed, they infect the rest, and that with increasing celerity."

So died Kempenfelt, one who never made an enemy, a character of deep religion, of high professional skill, and by no means the least distinguished among those of foreign blood who have contributed so much to the richness of England's story.

For close on a century a Kempenfelt had served the kingdom of his adoption. The father inspired enduring affection. The son did that and more; he proved that he could rise superbly to such rare opportunity as is granted to a junior sea commander.

Besides this, and with "the clear eye of a real master of war," as Corbett says, "he sought and found not a system of tactics but a system of evolutions." He was the brains of the Channel fleet for a brief but vital period when the command itself was in aged or shaky hands. He was versed in every side of his profession; the asides in his correspondence with Barham embrace everything from naval architecture, docking, discipline, and artillery to the making of rope. His remarks on the right age for command (and the wrong), on the handling of an inferior fleet faced by numbers, ring perennially true; while as long ago as 1779 he wrote, as if anticipating the true spirit of combined operations, "Our sea officers should be acquainted with the military art; the seamen and the soldier are two professions that should be united in the former."

12

DUNCAN AND THE FIGHT
AT CAMPERDOWN

THROUGH the centuries, and in spite of temporary
clouds, there has existed a special feeling of affection,
as well as of friendly rivalry, between the English
and the Dutch. Continental people though they are, with an
outlook acutely their own, the Dutch have long held an
Empire which has kept them sea-minded. They have maintained an efficient navy, used chiefly in overseas defence,
this being a legacy from a time when, as the Water Beggars,
they regained by commerce and the carrying-trade something
of the strength they had heroically dissipated in throwing
off the yoke of Spain. Never was theirs the narrowness of a
land-tied race. They still claim one of the proudest maritime
traditions in Europe.

Whenever in the past Holland and Britain have been
opposed, it has been a stubborn matter. The battles of the
Commonwealth, in which Blake won his immortality, were
among the fiercest ever known, and those of the Restoration
little less so. Those were the days of Tromp and de Ruyter,
to which every Dutchman looks back with pride. Their
triumphs are well remembered; nor has this nation ever
forgotten that dreadful year when, after laying up her capital
ships in a phase of financial stress, she heard Dutch guns
in the Thames and the Medway, and reached a peak of
humiliation never since surpassed. It is something to boast
of being the only nation ever to have made a successful
descent upon the London river. It is not so often recalled
that, over a century later, the Dutch were on the point of
trying another sortie, with French troops aboard their ships
to make a proper invasion of it. At that time, too, Holland

KEMPENFELT

Kempenfelt is holding an octagonal telescope. From a painting by Tilly Kettle in the National Maritime Museum, Greenwich

ranked as an occupied country, while Russia, as so lately, fought the tyrant of Europe at our side. The alliance was intermittent: Muscovite ships were not present, for instance, at the clash which decided the issue with Holland, but a squadron had lately been under British orders. The Admiral concerned was one who, though known to history, stands rather outside the classic line of sea commanders, and his most notable service, the victory of Camperdown, tends to be overlooked, since the great sea battles of the eighteenth century were lost and won mainly in the Atlantic or the Mediterranean. His name was Adam Duncan.

By birth a Scot, he was, like his father and grandfather before him, a man of splendid presence and physique. He stood six feet four, and his build was proportionate. He began his sea life in 1746, and spent his most formative years under the influence of Hawke. He had risen to post-rank early enough to play a leading part in the two great operations for the relief of Gibraltar; that conducted by Rodney in 1780, which included the engagement near Cape St. Vincent, and Howe's tactical feat of 1782. Duncan was a sterling captain, though he was not a leader of professional thought. Not for him the silent tussle that was waged behind the scenes all through the years of his activity to establish better ways of handling ships. There the spadework was done (largely by borrowing from French systems) by Howe, Kempenfelt, Barham, and to some degree Rodney. For his part, Duncan was content to accept the existing order of things. Yet his equipment was such as enabled him to seize the fleeting moment, to pursue the bold design, and he was clear-headed enough to recognize the genius which lay behind the leadership of his contemporary, Nelson. Courage was Duncan's strength, and in three ways did he display it. The first was by his handling of mutiny, which needed moral qualities as well as physical; the second was by his refusal to be daunted by long periods of unrewarded vigilance or thwarted by inadequate means; the third was that shown in a major encounter with a valiant enemy—his final reward and the dream of every sea commander.

The series of successes which followed the days of Matthews and Byng right down to Trafalgar sometimes raises the question how far they were due to native skill, how much to foreign weakness. French, Spanish, and Dutch showed no lack of bravery, that much is always conceded, while the French at any rate were at one time in the eighteenth century well ahead of the world in the theory of signals, evolutions and tactics, and in the design of ships. Their weakness was that they were beridden with the doctrine that the first duty of an Admiral is to keep his fleet intact rather than to seek a decision. Acceptance of such a theory has invariably led to catastrophe in conflicts with opponents prepared to risk all in attaining outright predominance. And that was the British way. It is true, therefore, that when facing an enemy, at any rate after the trial and execution of poor Byng in 1757 for his indecisive conduct before Minorca, the British fleet was generally fortified with that unseen but potent weapon, the will not merely to engage, but to destroy at all hazard. As it is a view which has seldom since been out of fashion, Byng may be said to have been a sacrifice in a great cause. He has indeed served to "encourage the others" by his drastic fate on the rare occasions when they have needed it.

If it be admitted that the Royal Navy always, at any rate after Quiberon, held the moral initiative, and if it also be true that—particularly with the Spanish—her Admirals often faced poorly managed squadrons, it cannot always be assumed that seamanlike perfection resided within her wooden walls, or that these were commanded by Nelsons. British seamen were sometimes scum, often pressed, and occasionally invalids swept by crisis from the hospitals. The individual captains were not always courageous, even though in general they were so; their grasp of tactics was often hazy; their ships were frequently inferior (St. Vincent's crack *Foudroyant*, a ship which Duncan also commanded, was, like many of the best, a prize); while general conditions in the service were so bad that once at least, and that at a time of peril, the fleet was in open mutiny. It was then that Duncan showed his greatness.

From his earliest days he had been a sympathetic leader, and in 1797, the year of crisis, he held command in the North Sea. His duty was to blockade the Texel, where the Dutch, compelled by the French, had assembled a menacing force of ships of the line and transports. Holland, then styled the Batavian Republic, was temporarily in opposition to the House of Orange, and was at the beck of Revolutionary France. Duncan, with his flag in the *Venerable*, and with a miscellaneous collection of ships under his orders, the discards from other commands, had learnt the importance and something of the art of blockade in Hawke's closure of Brest forty years before. Although he had spent much sea-time in his youth and had had a thorough grounding in his profession, long periods on half-pay followed, and he had risen by seniority rather than through experience in command of fleets to the position he occupied. He had no brilliant first captain to back his decisions and help resolve his problems, and it might have been expected that, like many other officers of merit, the mutinies which, starting at Spithead, spreading swiftly elsewhere, and finding their culmination under Richard Parker at the Nore, would have found him at a loss, particularly as his own forces lay so near the centre of trouble.

Like every other Admiral of the time, Duncan had personal dangers to face from his own seamen. His attitude to the disturbances, quaintly described by one of the men as "interesting though tumultuous proceedings," was a blend of the conciliatory approach by which, in his old age, Howe

was able to compose the men at Spithead, and of the stern-
ness of St. Vincent. His feeling for the men's grievances
was known to be genuine; equally firm was his insistence on
respect for his officers and his flag. His popularity, fairness,
and personal resolution made it sure that the fighting efficiency of his own ship would not be impaired, but it was
not possible for him to prevent the contagion from spreading
in others. In every case brought immediately before him,
he acted with decision. St. Vincent's way was to make a
ship's company execute their own ringleaders. It was brutal
but, with him, and on a foreign station, effective. Duncan's
threat was to hang those refusing duty with his own hand.
It was an action of which he looked fully capable; indeed,
in visiting the *Adamant*, then in a state of open insubordina-
tion, a particular seaman bade him defiance. He seized him
by the collar and held him over the side of the ship with his
outstretched arm. "My lads," he said to the assembled men,
"look at this fellow, he who dares to deprive me of command
of the fleet." They looked, and were impressed, but the
spirit of just grievance was so strong amongst the men
that individual captains, not always possessing either the
physique or the authority of Duncan, were unable to keep
their ships at their proper stations in the blockade. So much
was this true that at one time the threat to the Texel was
maintained by but two big ships, "cargoes of courage" if
ever there were such, backed by the usual bluff of signals
and lights to imaginary squadrons in the offing. Such
audacity has seldom been so outrageous or so necessary.
They were the *Vengeance* and the *Adamant*.

Fortunately, matters even within the Texel were not
without difficulty. The Dutch seamen were in little better
heart than the British mutineers; their pay was also in arrears,
relations with the French were strained, adherents of the
House of Orange made matters delicate. Moreover, the
enemy fleet had had no chance to practise manoeuvres.

The ships might be as stout as they were plentiful, but the proof would be upon the open sea. And so, for one reason and another, they did not venture forth at the one time when they could have done so with success, the only barrier then being an Admiral determined to fight his loyal ships to the last. No bluff ever succeeded better.

When the Dutch did appear, the whole balance of affairs had altered, and for the better. The mutiny was quelled, the ringleaders executed, and Duncan had under his orders a fleet of reasonable size, though it had had slender opportunities for knitting itself into a trained force. Ships and captains were still in the main a scratch lot, and this despite the affection and personal consideration he had from the First Lord, Spencer. It was late in the year, October, that the frigates reported the enemy at sea. Time and occasion do not seem to have been well chosen. The French army had dispersed; Dutch opinion in general had been opposed to venturing the ships, whose purpose in putting to sea at all appeared to be more of a gesture than part of a well-ordered strategic plan. The force was commanded by de Winter, a brave man but young—he was thirty-six—and one who, leaving the sea early, had spent all his active service as a soldier.

Brilliantly as they were shadowed by the light forces during their brief and ineffective cruise, and promptly as Duncan weighed with his ships of the line, the enemy nearly eluded him. The margin was indeed so narrow that the action, taking place within sight of the enemy coast on October 11, 1797, was fought in circumstances which permitted those of the enemy ships that lagged and hung fire, and some of those that were crippled in action, to reach the safety of their own shore batteries. The battle itself was as decisive as any fought during that period at sea. It was the spirit of Blake which triumphed in the last clash with these doughty antagonists of the Low Countries. The setting of the final scene was as dramatic as any in an age which appears in retrospect to have been as full in heroic incident as our own. At the time, Nelson was at home recuperating from the loss of his arm at Santa Cruz. Hearing rumours of the imminent battle, he exclaimed: "I would give this other arm to be with Duncan at this moment."

When the enemy were sighted, within easy distance of their own coast, the wind was blowing straight onshore. The Dutch formed their line boldly enough, but it was clear to Duncan that if he did not grapple promptly they would get into shoal water, when no attack would be possible. It was essential that Duncan should get between the enemy and the land. He had hoped to bring his fleet up in a compact body, for at best his numbers were not more than equal; but it was imperative that action should be joined at once, without waiting for the ships astern to come up, without indeed waiting to form line of battle. The order of sailing, which was irregular, was of two groups, one led by Duncan in the *Venerable* and the other by Onslow in the *Monarch*. Duncan made the signal to pass through the enemy's line and engage to leeward. After the first Dutch broadsides, which were devastating, the British, superior in training, fired three guns to their one. In all, some fifteen Dutch ships struck or were taken during the fight, but the damage to the British fleet was itself so severe, and the fire so hot, that no boats could be got away to take possession until the main engagement was over, by which time some had escaped. One of the ships most forward to distinguish herself was the *Belliqueuse*, where mutiny had formerly been particularly rife. Her captain was a Scot who like many another had neglected to make himself fully master of the Signal Book. At the crucial moment he threw it down upon the deck, exclaiming: "Up wi' the hel-lem and gang into the middle o't!" Another was the *Director*, commanded by Bligh of the *Bounty*.

Duncan has sometimes been blamed for his lack of tactical method. He could well simply have pointed to the results of the action, but his best justification comes from the mouth of his opponent. "Your not waiting to form the line," said de Winter, "ruined me; if I had got nearer to the shore and you had attacked, I should probably have drawn both fleets on it, and it would have been a victory to me, being on my own coast."

Battle was joined at 12.30 and ended at three, being fought with great stubbornness throughout. The British flagship had forty-five shot between wind and water. As for the Dutch, de Winter and his pilot were, of the deck officers of the *Vryheid*, alone unwounded. When Lieutenant Richardson of the *Circe* boarded, he found the Dutch Admiral on his knees on the quarter-deck, not in prayer, but holding a square sheet of lead which a carpenter was nailing over a shot hole in the bottom of a small punt about twelve feet long. In this the commander had been hoping to make his escape. While he was being taken across to the *Venerable*, a boatswain remarked that although de Winter was a big man he was going to meet a bigger. Duncan naturally treated his adversary with the fullest courtesy, both then and later. Offered the Dutchman's sword, he said, "I would much rather take a brave man's hand than his sword." De Winter's great sorrow was that he should have been the first Dutch Admiral to have surrendered on the scene of action, but he was spared all feeling of humiliation. Later, at a banquet in London, he appealed to Duncan for his judgment in the view that had he been better supported the story might have been different. Duncan's reply reveals him as a man of tact. "Sir," he said simply, "I am very happy to pledge your good health."

The carnage on both sides had been considerable. It is recorded that in one British ship, when a man had been killed at one of the lower guns, his place was taken by a woman, who soon afterwards had both her legs shattered.

Although there were many prizes taken, it occasioned remark that none of the Dutch vessels, even among those which could be successfully repaired, were afterwards taken into the British service. It was enough that they were out of action. The relief from the protracted threat from the eastern quarter was widespread and vocal. Feeling ran high throughout the country. A clear victory is always a tonic, and in the autumn of 1797 one was badly needed. The public view was well summed up in a letter written by a seaman soon after the battle. "They say," he said, "as how they are going to make a lord of the Admiral. They can't make too much of him. He is heart of oak; he is a seaman every inch of him, and as to a bit of a broadside, it only makes the old cock young again."

The seaman's news was true. Duncan was made a Viscount, and received the Freedom of many cities. His welcome home was especially warm in his native Scotland, to which he finally retired, full of years and honour, in 1800, to enjoy anew those pleasures of family life with which his long periods on half-pay had made him familiar. He died in 1804, modest, serene, and God-fearing as he had always lived.

"The name of Duncan," wrote Nelson when he heard the news, "will not soon be forgot by Britain, and in particular by its Navy." King William IV, that jovial sailor whose eccentricities and kindness of heart were never predictable, was of the same opinion. No doubt he recalled his own service as a midshipman in the *Royal George*, when he had been a fellow-officer with Duncan in Rodney's fleet. In 1831, when he had power to do so, William raised the dignity bestowed for Camperdown to an Earldom. The honour was extant for just over a century.

THE *ROYAL GEORGE*

Stern view showing Admiral's and Captain's gallery, from a contemporary model in the National Maritime Museum, Greenwich

13

BILLY BLUE: CORNWALLIS

Fortify your mind against all misfortunes and disappointments, and be as happy as you can.
LORD CORNWALLIS *to his brother, October* 14, 1764.

I

OF all the celebrated commanders of the past, it would have surprised Cornwallis least to find himself forgotten. Very much of a piece with his life, he would have thought it, full of great possibilities, great expectations and—great disappointments. It is not given to many to be famous chiefly for a retreat, yet it is for such an action that historians of naval tactics rate him high. Few faced (and outfaced) so many redoubtable opponents in the course of a mortal span. Cornwallis also had the honour and responsibility of being at the head of his country's principal fleet at one of the four great crises in its history, and played a part in another. Last but far from least, he inspired the friendship and gratitude of Nelson. A man well remembered in the navy, but very little outside it, he was a leader of mettle and, through trying years, held the general confidence.

The peaks of danger from without, so far as the modern history of this land is concerned, are widely admitted to have been 1588, the year of the Armada; 1759, the year of Quiberon Bay; 1805, the year of Trafalgar; and 1940. It was the second of these thrilling occasions, Hawke's victory over Conflans, won amid the crash of surf upon rock and the roar of a November gale, which first began to entrench a tradition of combat supremacy never since to be lost in European waters. Cornwallis had the luck to serve in the

Dunkirk in this action as a boy of fifteen, and there grew within him a conviction, not afterwards modified, that mastery at sea could be certain, whatever the odds, as long as the chief commander thought and acted with a wise boldness. He infected others. In the year before he died Nelson wrote to him: "I feel that I imbibed from you certain sentiments which have greatly assisted me in my naval career—that we could always beat a Frenchman if we fought him long enough."

Many men later renowned fought at Quiberon; Howe, Rodney, and Alexander Hood among them; it was a battle which, besides saving the country from the most serious threat of invasion it was to know until the advent of Napoleon, left enduring marks upon all who took part in it. It became a pattern for emulation, as did Hawke's whole tenacious policy of blockade.

Besides starting his active service under one of the greatest captains, the young Cornwallis had other advantages. He was the son of an earl and brother to a man who, as Governor-General of India, became a marquis. He had, moreover, an ambitious and persevering mother; nor was he ever handicapped by a too narrow purse. It was to be expected, therefore, that he would reach post rank young. He did so, being but twenty-one when he was given command of the *Prince Edward*. Nelson, it will be recalled, was made post at the same early age. Both men served long as captains or commodores before they gained Admiral's status; Nelson for eighteen years, Cornwallis for twenty-eight, though for much of this time both held independent command.

A considerable part of Cornwallis's earlier years was spent in the West Indies, which in the eighteenth century had an importance hard to over-estimate. They were the scene of protracted and major contests between the English and the French, with Spanish, Dutch, and Danes ready to participate at critical times. Cornwallis fought at the battle of Grenada in 1779 under Byron, in command of the *Lion*. Byron showed himself an Admiral of more haste than skill. He flew precipitately into battle without waiting to form line. Cornwallis was badly mauled, being without support, and narrowly escaped destruction, with his ship. The *Lion* was dismasted and cut off from the squadron, and should have been an easy prey to D'Estaing, who, however, hesitated to attack. Cornwallis went off successfully before the wind under such sail as could be set on the stumps of the lower masts.

Less than a year later, cruising alone near Monte Christi, he fell in with a French convoy escorted by four ships of the line and a frigate under La Motte Picquet. These gave chase, and brought him to action. The engagement continued intermittently all day, without conclusion despite the great odds; but when the *Ruby*, an English 64 with two frigates, came in sight, the French sheered off. Three months later Cornwallis came upon de Ternay with nine of the line and a frigate, escorting de Rochambeau's troops to North America. Although Cornwallis had but two ships of 64, two of 50, with one frigate, de Ternay did not attempt to overwhelm him, but drew away after a desultory exchange of fire. Cornwallis's was already a name redoubtable to the enemy.

It was still as a captain, then with many years of sea experience behind him, that he served in another battle which has made some noise in history, Rodney's victory over de Grasse in 1782, the battle of the Saints, where, it has been held, the line was first broken with success. There has been such dispute about this, and about the fight as a whole, that it is pertinent to recall that even Rodney was at first uncertain whether he should expect praise or blame for his conduct of the action. That it was praise and honours which befell him was partly owing to the political situation at home. The Administration needed victories, and here was one to hand. The credit did not extent to the individual captains, for whom Rodney had scant praise. Opinion in the service, vigorously shared by Hood and Nelson, was that it was an affair which, had it been pursued, would have been among the most glorious in naval annals, but that it was hard to speak of it without disappointment. So felt Cornwallis, though loyalty to Rodney made him circumspect in saying so. He had now learnt two major lessons in action: one was the magic of courage, the other the mortification felt if an advantage was incompletely followed up.

It was on his way home from a spell of duty in the West Indies that Cornwallis grew intimate with Nelson who, at the time a sick man, took passage in the *Lion*. In many later letters Nelson contrived to convey that sense of affection he always felt for his colleague. Three years later, in 1789, when Cornwallis was given charge of the East Indies Station, his brother then being established at Calcutta, Nelson would have welcomed the chance of serving in his squadron. Cornwallis hesitated to disturb what he thought was Nelson's happy domesticity in Norfolk, and the opportunity passed.

The circumstances of Cornwallis's time in the East did not tend to glory at sea. For the most part French and British were nominally at peace, at all times likely to be broken; for friction was continuous and considerable. The two brothers enjoyed their service in India; Marquis Cornwallis gained fame and no small fortune; Commodore Cornwallis always spoke of the station with some pleasure, though, if William Hickey is to be believed, it was not good for his temper. Hickey met him in 1790, and did not like him. "The Commodore," he wrote, "is a living Trunion, but more of a brute than Smollett made his hero."

Cornwallis returned to England in 1794. He had been made a Rear-Admiral the year before, and was promoted Vice-Admiral in the July after his return. In June 1795 he fought his memorable retreat. While on service of blockade, his flag flying in the *Royal Sovereign* of 100 guns, and with four 74s and two frigates in company, he was faced once more with what he already knew so well. He encountered off Brest a French fleet of twelve of the line, with many large frigates and small craft, all under the command of Villaret Joyeuse. Two of the English ships, the *Bellerophon* and *Brunswick*, were heavy sailers; and this gave the French time to form up in two divisions, one on each quarter of Cornwallis's force. The first sighting was made on June 16th. On the morning of the 17th brisk interchange of shot took place between the French van and the English rearguard, where the *Mars* suffered much in her rigging. So greatly was she in peril that Cornwallis wore round his flagship to her support, a manoeuvre which so astonished the French that they thought the main British fleet must be in the offing. Cornwallis's tactics were supported by that skilful deception employed so well by Duncan off the Texel, and by Harwood off the Plate: dispositions and signals designed to give the impression that the squadron was expecting immediate support.

Cornwallis saved the *Mars* and all her consorts. He returned home with the vital intelligence that the enemy were at sea in force, and with a reputation for his conduct of the action that placed him high in the estimation of a profession which then included St. Vincent and Howe, Duncan and Bridport, Pellew and Nelson, and other names famous in history. "Remember," were his orders to the *Royal Sovereign's* company, "flag and ensign are never to be struck to an enemy. She goes down with them flying."

After the action Barham wrote from Whitehall: "I have read your journal with the utmost satisfaction, and it is proposed to bind it up separate, to be kept at the Admiralty as a model of professional conduct."

Villaret Joyeuse, incidentally, deserves to be remembered

for his decision, made in 1803, not to employ the submarine device invented by the American Fulford, as being contrary to his ideas of "civilized warfare."

II

Not a year after his retreat Cornwallis was in trouble with the Admiralty for almost the first and last time in his career. He had been appointed Commander-in-Chief in the West Indies, and sailed to his new post in the *Royal Sovereign*, covering a convoy. Unfortunately, a transport fouled the flagship soon after leaving England, and damaged her so severely that Cornwallis decided she must return. He himself stayed in her, and added to official disapproval by refusing to take up his command in a frigate placed at his disposal. Although his health was bad at this time, Cornwallis was utterly in the wrong, and the Admiralty took the only course. They court-martialled him. The court's verdict was that he should have transferred his flag to another ship at sea, and have proceeded. As a result of this trial he was relieved of a command which he never wished to assume.

Five years later, Cornwallis took over the Channel fleet from St. Vincent, and began that watch and ward which frustrated Napoleon and turned the Emperor's eyes towards the abyss of the Russian campaign. The storm-tossed ships, exercising the relentless pressure of blockade, are honoured in story, as they should be. Their service was as arduous and often as ill-rewarded as it was important. Cornwallis in his great days as Commander-in-Chief was a man approaching sixty, yet so eager was he that his nick-name, "Billy Blue," derived from his custom of flying the Blue Peter whenever his vessels were driven into Torbay by stress of weather. He had another, "Billy-go-Tight,"; for although no sot, and on duty severe in his habits, he was as fond of his glass as any seaman at that time. The life made need of compensa-

tions. "Collingwood prefers cold to wet," he remarked in
1804. "Both are bad when you can retire from neither."
And a glimpse of the principal pleasures to be anticipated
from respite may be had from a note sent to Cornwallis
by a bum-boat woman when his ship, the *Ville de Paris*,
arrived off Spithead. "Mrs. Carey presents her compliments
to Admiral Cornwallis," this runs. "She is alongside the
Ville de Paris with a Bottle of Gin, a Brown Loaf, a pot of
Fresh Butter, a Basket of Garden stuff, and a pint of Rich
Cream. If the Commander-in-Chief will not receive her and
Party, she will immediately dash off to some of the Young
Captains."

Cornwallis's period in command of the Channel fleet
included the time of Nelson's Trafalgar campaign. Cornwallis
had, indeed, spared his old friend the *Victory* in 1803 ("It
was like yourself," wrote Nelson in gratitude, "and very
unlike many others which you and I know"), and on Nelson's
return home for the last time he brought Cornwallis some
gifts from the West Indies.

In March 1806 St. Vincent returned to the Channel
Command, and Cornwallis had no more service afloat. He
spent his retirement on his estate of Newlands, to which he
gave devoted care. His pleasures were hardy. "He rose at
four o'clock," recorded Miss Whitby, daughter of his old
flag-captain, who with her mother spent the later years with
him, "and rode out on his favourite pony from six to eight
in all weathers and seasons. Then to breakfast. The meal
was very simple. One half cup of strong green tea and
innocent of milk and sugar, a thick piece of bread, which he
himself toasted and ate without butter. A plain lunch at
one, and dinner at six, and always drank his bottle of port.
Strong coffee, a game of bagatelle, and to bed."

When the authorities were compiling an honours list
at the end of the war in 1815 they remembered the old
Admiral, and made him a G.C.B. He enjoyed this belated

knighthood four years, and may well have reflected that Hawke had had to wait seventeen years for the peerage which should at once have rewarded Quiberon Bay. Cornwallis died in 1819. He has had but one biographer, Major Cornwallis West, who records that his last words, spoken to a child, were, "My dear, my dear, God bless you always!" His wish was granted, though that same child put up a monument to his memory which he expressly preferred to be without.

14

NELSON'S BLACKWOOD

I

NELSON'S cry, as all remember, was for frigates. It is the call of every aggressive admiral, though the name changes. The fleet needs eyes, and these must interpret quickly, with intelligence. Although he seldom had enough, three years before Trafalgar Nelson recognized a captain able to handle frigates after his own style. His name was Henry Blackwood.

Fame has linked the two men, but their association was brief in point of time. As late as April 5, 1802, when Blackwood was a post-captain, Nelson wrote to him from Palermo: "Is there a sympathy which ties men together in the bonds of friendship without having a personal knowledge of each other? If so (and, I believe, it was so to you), I was your friend and acquaintance before I saw you."

The occasion of this letter was one of the best actions Blackwood ever fought. He was in command of the *Penelope*, 36, one of several ships bearing illustrious names with which his name is joined, and was engaged in the blockade of Malta, then held by Napoleon. There he fell in with the *Guillaume Tell*, a French capital ship of 80 guns wearing the flag of Admiral Decres. She was a survivor from the fleet defeated at Aboukir. Blackwood's frigate sighted and pursued her. In a long chase he brought down her main-topmast, the reduction in speed thus effected enabling St. Vincent's old ship the *Foudroyant*—herself a French prize—and the *Lion* to defeat her. "Your conduct and character," said Nelson of this affair, "stamps your fame beyond the reach of envy: it was like yourself—it was like the *Penelope*. Thanks;

and say every kind thing for me to your brave officers and men."

None were warmer in praise of Blackwood than the chivalrous Decres, who acknowledged his masterly seamanship. The two became friends, a circumstance which may have owed something to the fact that Blackwood, like Kempenfelt before him, had been at pains to learn what he could from France and in France. He spent 1792 at Angoulême and Paris, learnt the language thoroughly, and witnessed the September massacres, after which he wisely fled.

Blackwood's seamanship was acquired in a stern school. He joined the *Artois* frigate in 1781 at the tender age of eleven, and was present at Sir Hyde Parker's action of the Dogger Bank against the Dutch, a quick taste of battle. After service in other frigates, and a spell as signal midshipman with Lord Howe in the *Queen Charlotte*, came his visit to France, his naval career being resumed as lieutenant in the *Active*. In July 1793 came an appointment to a larger ship, the *Invincible*, 74, where he was first lieutenant. He had the good fortune to serve in the *Invincible* in Howe's victory of the Glorious First of June. His ship engaged the *Juste*, 84, a much larger vessel, and in half an hour so damaged her as to cause her to fall prey to the *Queen Charlotte*. Blackwood was ordered to take possession, and was promoted for his part in the battle.

In April 1796 he was given command of the *Brilliant*, 28, in Duncan's motley North Sea force then blockading the Texel. He missed Camperdown, being ordered to the Newfoundland station before that decisive clash. In July 1798 his ship fought a most unequal contest near Santa Cruz with two French frigates, *La Vertu* and *La Regenerée*. Although inconclusive, the *Brilliant* came off with small loss and great credit. St. Vincent, a man not given to cheap praise, spoke of it as an engagement "in which Captain Blackwood has displayed great valour and judgment, and acquired great renown." The practical result was his appointment to the *Penelope*, which he commanded with such vigour in the Mediterranean.

Blackwood left the *Penelope* in 1802, and, in the year following, St. Vincent gave him the *Euryalus* of the same rating. In this ship he served throughout the Trafalgar campaign. His first task was to trace the movements of the fleets under Villeneuve and Gravina after their brush with Calder off Finisterre. He watched them into Cadiz, then raced for England with news of their whereabouts. He reached home in five days, enabling Barham to make those dispositions which were to result in Nelson's final victory. He called at Merton on his way to London, arriving at five in the morning and finding Nelson already up and dressed. "I am sure," said Nelson, "you bring me news of the French and Spanish fleets, and I think I shall yet have to beat them."

Nelson followed him to London, and the two were never afterwards far apart. On September 29, 1805, Nelson appointed Blackwood to the command of the Inshore Squadron off Cadiz, a post of honour if ever there was one. The squadron consisted of five frigates and four sloops. Nelson had offered him a big ship, indeed a choice of several, including the crack *Revenge*, but Blackwood declined. He had made his reputation in smaller vessels, and intended for the present to stick to the *Euryalus*. For one thing, he did not at first believe that Villeneuve would face Nelson. "They will not budge," he wrote to England, "unless forced out by blockade. Such a fleet as Lord Nelson will have in another week, indeed as he has already, England never sent out before."

From the time of his appointment as Inshore Commodore until the day before the battle, while Nelson kept station from thirteen to twenty leagues west of Cadiz, Blackwood stuck close to the enemy port. "I am confident," wrote Nelson on October 4th, "you will not let these gentry slip through our fingers, and then we shall give a good account of them, although they may be very superior in numbers." Four days later he wrote again: "I am gratified (because it shows your soul is in your business) and obliged by all your communications. I see you feel how much my heart is set on getting at these fellows, whom I have hunted so long." He wrote again next day, and on the next, and again on the 14th. At last, at half-past nine on the morning of the 19th, Blackwood signalled that the enemy were coming out. Next day Nelson was informed that nearly forty sail had been seen "outside of Cadiz," and Nelson, fearing above all things that the fleet might pass the straits into the Mediterranean during the night, which promised to be dark and squally, made the following signal to Blackwood by Popham's telegraph: "I rely on you that I do not miss the enemy." Blackwood thereupon brought his own ship to within half a gunshot of the one which he guessed carried the French admiral.

The same day he wrote to his wife that the sight and prospect was "magnificently beautiful. I expect before this hour to-morrow to carry General Decres on board the *Victory* in my barge, which I have just painted nicely for him." He thought his old opponent was with the French fleet, though this was not so.

On the morning of Trafalgar he was summoned to the flagship. His hope was then, battle being imminent, to be given command of one of the big ships which were without captains. Nelson told him, indeed, that he had intended to transfer him to the *Ajax* or the *Thunderer*, but that on reflection he thought that Blackwood could render more essential service in command of the light squadron. Nelson knew his man and his record, and who can doubt that his decision was right?

Blackwood stayed five and a half hours on board the *Victory*, and did not leave the flagship until the enemy had opened fire. He witnessed Nelson's will, and the peerless little man's last words to him are famous. "God bless you, Blackwood—I shall never see you more."

II

Although Blackwood had not known Nelson long he had, like everyone else, fallen under his spell. As soon as he could snatch a few moments to write to his wife he told her: "A victory, and such a one as was never before achieved, took place yesterday in the course of five hours; but at such an expense, in the loss of the most gallant of men— the best and kindest of friends, as renders it to me a victory I could hardly have ever wished to witness on such terms. . . . They were attacked in a way no other Admiral ever before conceived an idea of. . . ."

As he wrote, Collingwood, who had succeeded Nelson in command, was on board the *Euryalus*, his own ship being dismasted. Then came the sad loss of the prizes through the exigencies of the weather and the state of the battered ships. Blackwood himself, to his great regret, was forced to destroy the *Santissima Trinidada*, a vessel of 100 guns. On October 25th he wrote to his wife: "The French Commander-in-Chief, Villeneuve, is at this moment at my elbow; he was brought hither yesterday from one of our ships. . . . Dear must Lord Nelson's memory ever be to all. His place as an Admiral cannot, in my opinion, ever be filled up. Hitherto my head from employment has been in such a gale of wind, that I have not been able to devote a thought almost to the loss of such a friend. On the day of action, he not only gave me the command of all the frigates for the purpose of assisting disabled ships, but he also gave me a latitude seldom or ever given—that of making any use I pleased of his name in ordering any of the sternmost line-of-battle ships to do what struck me as best. I wish to

God he had yielded to my entreaties to come on board my ship."

He continued: "Villeneuve says he never saw anything like the irresistible fire of our ships; but that of the *Victory*, supported by *Neptune* and *Temeraire*, was what he could not have formed any judgment of; but I did what I could to render him and his ships all the service in my power during the heat of the action. I went down among them all, and took the *Royal Sovereign* in tow, which enabled him to keep his broadside on the enemy; all of this without firing a shot from *Euryalus*, which was difficult to prevent, but had I permitted it, I could not have performed the service."

Blackwood much wished to be sent home with despatches. Collingwood fulfilled this natural desire, and in a circumstantial letter referred to him as follows: "The *Royal Sovereign* having lost her masts, excepting the tottering foremast, I called the *Euryalus* to me, while the action yet continued, which ship lying within hail, made my signals, a service which Captain Blackwood performed with great attention. After that action I shifted my flag to her, that I might more easily communicate my orders, and towed the *Royal Sovereign* out to eastward." The *Euryalus* carried Admirals Villeneuve and Majendie to England, and Blackwood himself was enabled to attend Nelson's funeral at St. Paul's. He was trainbearer to the Admiral of the Fleet, Nelson's old patron, Sir Peter Parker. Although Blackwood's place in the temple of fame was now assured, the remainder of his active service must in some measure have seemed an anticlimax, though it did not lack excitement.

In 1806 Barham appointed him to the *Ajax*, 80. He joined Lord Collingwood in the Mediterranean on the anniversary of Trafalgar, but his tenure in command of this first big ship was brief. She was intended to form part of a squadron under Sir John Duckworth in an expedition against Constantinople, but on February 14, 1807, at the mouth of the

Straits, disaster befell her. Fire broke out in the bread-room, where the purser's steward and his mate lay drunk. This fire, despite all Blackwood's efforts, spread so fast that the ship was burnt out, with the loss of almost half her company. Thanks to Blackwood's own exertions, the magazine was flooded and explosion did not immediately add to the horrors of the night, though she blew up later with a mighty report near to the spot where Ajax himself was buried. The captain was exonerated at the inquiry which followed. "It was proved," ran the verdict, "that every possible precaution had been taken before the fire was discovered, and after it every possible exertion used by Captain Blackwood for the preservation of the ship." He was later formally acquitted by court martial. As he wrote to his wife: "Though unfortunate, I am not disgraced."

After the disaster Blackwood served as volunteer in the flagship, the *Royal George* (successor to Kempenfelt's), in Duckworth's abortive expedition. He was then sent home with despatches. He refused an offer of a post at the Navy Board, and was given the *Warspite*, 74, in which he served in the North Sea, the Channel, and finally the Mediterranean.

In July 1810, off Toulon, he fought his last action. The *Warspite* had in company the *Ajax*, *Conqueror*, *Euryalus*, and a brig—ships whose names he knew well of old—when six sail of the line appeared under a Vice-Admiral. Their task was to free a French man-of-war with her convoy which was held by the British force in Bandol. The French, though so greatly superior in numbers, were prevented from their purpose, Blackwood reporting to his Commander-in-Chief: "From the determined conduct of the squadron you did me the honour to place under my command, I am fully per-suaded, had the ambition of the enemy permitted him to make a bolder attack, the result would have been still more favourable to His Majesty's arms."

Blackwood served in the Mediterranean under Sir Charles

Cotton and Lord Exmouth—the latter another great frigate captain—until 1812, when he returned to England for the repair of his ship. The remainder of his six years in command was spent in blockade, first off the Scheldt, then off Brest, and Rochfort. When he relinquished his appointment in November 1813 he could fairly say that with the exception of ten months at the peace of Amiens, he had been on active service, without any blemish to his public or private character and under some of the most distinguished commanders, for no less than thirty-two years and eight months, "in the course of which I was engaged, either as Lieutenant or Captain, in some of the most celebrated actions in both wars."

The rest of Blackwood's life was mere honour and glory. In 1814 the Duke of Clarence, later William IV, made him captain of the fleet assembled to bring over the newly restored Bourbons to this country on a ceremonial visit. After the naval review at Portsmouth which followed he was made a baronet, and he achieved his Flag. Five years later he was appointed Commander-in-Chief, East Indies. On the way out, in the *Leander*, he was nearly wrecked off Madeira, in Funchal Road. The captain of the ship, Richardson, managed to wear in the nick of time, and Blackwood was wont to say that in all his time at sea he never felt so near despair. In 1827 he was given command at the Nore, the last of a long and honourable sequence of appointments.

Blackwood died in 1832, being then a Vice-Admiral, and with a career behind him which has assured him immortality. The navy before his day and since has produced many fine leaders of light forces. Blackwood's luck was to have been the right man in the right place at one of the peaks of glory.

ALGECIRAS

Saumarez prepares. From a print after Brenton in the National Maritime Museum, Greenwich

15

KEATS AND THE *SUPERB*

THE greater number of sea commanders would agree that, at any rate until lately, the most perplexing part of naval warfare lay within the sphere of the night action. The prime difficulty is to distinguish friend from foe, and if curiosity be prompted to inquire whether damage on a great scale has ever been self-inflicted, the fullest answer is perhaps found in an encounter of H.M.S. *Superb* in 1801, when she was commanded by Richard Keats. It is one of the most extraordinary stories in naval history.

Keats left a record of the action in the hands of Jervis's secretary, Tucker, which was afterwards published by Tucker's son. At the time the *Superb* was serving with a squadron under Saumarez based at Gibraltar, its main purpose to blockade Cadiz. Saumarez had met with and attacked a French force at Algeciras on July 6th, but had been repulsed with the loss of the *Hannibal*, and with many casualties in other vessels, due to the fire of shore batteries. The *Superb*, which had been left to watch Cadiz, then rejoined him, driven before a Spanish force which left the port. French and Spanish now combined, while Saumarez made superhuman efforts at quick repair. On the 12th the enemy left Algeciras, confident that the English had had such a battering that they could slip away unmolested, though they much outnumbered Saumarez and might have annihilated him. Instead, Saumarez pursued them. With a fresh easterly wind his ships became scattered, and about nine o'clock, with little daylight remaining, the *Superb*, which was then new from England, was ordered to attack the enemy's rear, keeping inshore.

The *Superb* set her courses and top-gallant sails, and quickly drew away from her consorts, overtaking the enemy in the gathering dusk at a speed of between eleven and twelve knots. "About this time," says Keats, "I ordered the first and second captains of the guns to be assembled on the quarter-deck. I then told them that I had had the advantage of having been in action with the enemy by night, and predicted to them what precisely took place—namely, that the Spaniards would blow up, and that we should have more to apprehend from our own carelessness of powder, than from any efforts of the enemy." Prescient as he was, even Keats could not have anticipated the extraordinary events of the night.

The master, and a "trusty, steady seaman" called Sutherland M'Beth, whom Keats described as the best look-out he ever knew, soon confirmed that the ship nearest them, with which they would first engage, was a three-decker which afterwards proved to be the Spanish *Real Carlos*, 112, of most formidable size. At about half-past eleven Keats fired a broadside into this ship. She was utterly surprised. The captain and other officers were dining in the cabin, and the first and last which many of the party knew of battle was the arrival of English shot. This was not the worst. Part of the *Superb's* fire flew beyond the *Real Carlos* and hit the *San Heremenegildo*, whose station was on her seaward side. Thinking the shots came from the *Real Carlos* and that she was hostile, the *San Hermenegildo*, whose gunnery was keener than her recognition, discharged into her consort, and within a few moments the wretched *Real Carlos* was engaged from two directions. When she herself began to reply, her fire was ragged and ineffectual.

It was soon apparent to Keats that he need concern himself no more with the two great ships. They would dispatch one another. This they did with devastating thoroughness, falling behind the rest of the fleet, to be lost in fire and explosion, with great expense of life.

Having discharged two valedictory salvos, Keats sailed on to encounter the *St. Antoine*, 74, which he attacked with such steadiness and skill that at about thirty-five minutes after midnight the enemy struck. Her surrender was clear enough to the *Superb*. It was not so to two other ships, the *Cæsar*, Saumarez's flagship, and the *Formidable*, which continued to pound the unfortunate vessel until the mistake was all too apparent. Soon afterwards a boat-load of survivors from the *Real Carlos* and the *San Hermenegildo* were descried. They were taken on board the *Superb* and were assured, according to the courtesy of the day, that at least their sorrows would not be added to by their being treated as prisoners of war.

Saumarez gave Keats's conduct all the credit it deserved. He had redeemed the Admiral's discomfiture with a victory; for the enemy, routed, were chased into Cadiz, and Saumarez gained great honour from the fight. Saumarez, in Keats's words, "received me himself, at the gangway, and said aloud that he could not find language to express his sense of the services I had rendered to my country the last night." In his report of the action Keats said to Saumarez that he hoped he had not made too much of the services of his ship. "That is impossible," said the Admiral.

Such was the most memorable feat of the *Superb*. She was not always so fortunate. Two years later she joined Nelson off Toulon. Nelson welcomed Keats warmly, recognizing a kindred spirit, as he had done in Blackwood. Within three days he was writing of him as "one of the very best officers in His Majesty's navy. . . . I esteem his person alone as equal to one French 74, and the *Superb* and her captain equal to two 74-gun ships." This was flattering, but in fact the *Superb* had now been long due for refit, and in the chase to the West Indies she had always to be under press of canvas, the studding-sail booms lashed to the yards. Nelson saw this, and acknowledged Keats's devotion. "Be assured," he wrote, "that I know and feel that the *Superb* does all which it is possible for a ship to accomplish."

When the fleet returned to England she was forced to dock, and so missed Trafalgar. To Keats, who had endured so much and so long, it was a grievous blow. As the *Superb* sailed to join the fleet after her refit she met the *Pickle* off Land's End, bringing Collingwood's despatch. "What news?" she hailed. "Nineteen of the enemy taken and Lord Nelson killed." A deep groan came from the ship's company; many openly shed tears.

Her next service was as the flagship of Sir John Duckworth. The *Superb* took him to the West Indies, where she fought in the victory at San Domingo of February 1806. In this fight a band on the poop played "God Save the King" and "Nelson and the Nile." Keats brought out a picture of the hero, which he hung on the mizen stay. A seaman was killed beside it. He was not so lucky as another member of the company, a fine cockerel. A 42-lb. double-headed shot, smashing through the poultry-coop, destroyed all the fowls but this one bird. He flew up from the wreckage to the spanker-boom, crowing defiantly. Another shot smashed the boom in two close to his feet, but the doughty creature found another spar, where he continued crowing all through the fight. He was later seen to have lost an eye, and to have been bruised all over, but he survived. The Admiral presented him to the crew as a pet. They decorated him with rings and ribbons and found him a good home ashore, where he lived long in honoured retirement, no doubt boring his hens with stories of the wars.

Keats left his old ship in 1807 to serve as commodore in the *Ganges* in Baltic waters. But in the year following, after his promotion to Rear-Admiral, he returned to her, commanding a squadron in the Great Belt. There he seized some ten thousand Spaniards out of Danish merchantmen. These were men pressed into the French service in a way with which Europe has since been made all too familiar. They were released and sent home.

In 1809 the *Superb* paid off, Keats transferring to the *Implacable*, sailing in her to command a squadron off Cadiz. He saw two more years of war, serving at the last under Pellew, his own flag in the *Hibernia* off Toulon; then, his health impaired, he returned home, and to less active employment, first in Newfoundland and then as Governor of Greenwich Hospital. As for the *Superb*, she survived to do great things in Pellew's bombardment of Algiers in 1816.

Keats's death in 1834 was the occasion of eulogy from his profession. He was a "seaman's seaman." His reputation also owed something to the fact that the reigning sovereign in his last years was William IV, between whom and Keats there existed affection stretching back over half a century to the time when Keats had been a lieutenant in the *Prince George* and William midshipman of his watch. They had been shipmates two years, had served together at the relief of Gibraltar, and when Keats was appointed to the *Lion* and later to independent command, William had continued an interest which time was to transmute from that of admiring subordinate to that of powerful patron. It was at William's request that Keats had attained post rank in 1789. Four years later he had been appointed to the *London*, which was fitting out for William's flag. In the event he never hoisted it, and the ship was paid off, but the choice of captain was significant. William never forgot him. He commissioned a bust of Keats by Chantrey which commemorates a lasting friendship.

16

CAPTAIN CHAMIER AND BYRON

I

FIVE years after Trafalgar, the navy was in the midst of one of those tedious periods in its history when, although the main enemy had been defeated at sea, the war was not yet over, and the prospect lay before it of dull routine service, followed by inevitable reduction of establishment. Excitement was welcome, particularly to the young, and to a midshipman, Frederick Chamier by name, the year 1810 brought a sight of Byron. His youthful picture is vivid, moreover the meeting probably helped to turn his own thoughts to letters, and that to some profit, since in later years he wrote a popular novel of the sea—*Tom Bowling*.

Chamier was at the time a boy of fourteen, serving on the frigate *Salsette* in the Mediterranean. The life was hard; but he had already seen service with the Walcharen Expedition, had taken part in the capture of a prize, and had learnt to record what he saw with an eye for detail which makes his long-neglected autobiography, *The Life of a Sailor*, a store of information concerning the life of the navy immediately after Nelson.

It was at Smyrna, while watching a realistic sham fight between some Turks and Mamelukes, that Chamier first saw Byron. The *Salsette* had been ordered from Smyrna to Constantinople, where she was to receive the English minister and thence convey him to Malta. Byron, who was then with Hobhouse on his grand tour, solicited a passage to the Porte, which was gladly granted by the captain, one Bathurst, an amiable man with an engaging stammer.

Off the island of Tenedos, in view of the plains of Troy, Chamier began a direct acquaintance. "An orange brought me into notice with his lordship," he wrote. Byron had inquired of the captain's steward if such a luxury was to be procured on board; the steward answered that he had none. "I immediately ran below," says Chamier, "and from the till of my chest brought forth two ripe Smyrna oranges. Being well aware how the stall-women polish their fruit, by means of their lips and a blacking brush, I concluded a damp towel would answer every purpose, and having duly heightened the yellow skin of my fruit, returned and offered them."

The acquaintance quickly ripened. Next day Byron asked that he might be landed on the plains of Troy, at which he had been gazing for hours through a telescope. The captain agreed. "I will take this young acquaintance of mine with me, with your permission, Captain Bathurst," said Byron, and in a few minutes a gig took them ashore, Byron with a fowling-piece on his shoulder.

"Troy and its plains were hallowed ground to his lordship," wrote Chamier, "which I ventured to profane, by blazing away at every bird I saw; and while the poet was imagining the great events of former days, I was lost in sweet hope of the next day's dinner."

Byron, having explored the line of the old walls, "brought himself to anchor upon the tomb of Patrochus," and read Homer, "occasionally glancing his quick eye over the plains." He was much amused by Chamier's leaping across the Scamander, then a mere rivulet. Having crossed to Tenedos, tasted sherbet, and smoked a pipe with the governor, the pair returned on board the same evening.

So dilatory were the Turkish authorities in according Captain Bathurst the necessary firman to pass the forts of the Dardanelles that the *Salsette* was a whole month at anchor. Many excursions were made on shore, the longest being a ride to Abydos, in which Byron and his party took part, together with Bathurst and other officers. The poor captain did not get far. He had a disagreement with his horse, was seriously bruised, and was brought back to the frigate by Byron's servants.

Chamier was left under Byron's special care, and rode close by his side. About four miles inland they met a party of Turks, gorgeously clothed and mounted, and ready for instant battle with the unbelievers. "Had it not been for Byron's coolness," wrote Chamier, "we should have been minus a head or two before long." The poet was able to establish the good intentions of his party, which ultimately arrived safely at Abydos. Here they were greeted by a grumbling English consul (by nationality an Italian Jew), and proceeded thence by boat to Sestos, on the European shore.

It was then that Byron made his first attempt at imitating Leander, rubbing himself over with oil and taking to the water like a duck. On first plunging in he complained of the coldness, but he swam well—decidedly well. The current was strong, the wind high, and the waves unpleasant. These were stout odds to contend with, and when he arrived about half way across, he gave up the attempt, was handed into the boat, and dressed.

"He did not appear in the least fatigued," says Chamier, "but looked as cold as charity, and as white as snow. He was cruelly mortified at the failure, and did not speak one word until he arrived on shore. His look was that of an angry, disappointed girl, and his upper lip curled, like that of a passionate woman."

Having seen the town of Sestos, such as it was, the party hired another boat and sailed down the Dardanelles to the frigate. Chamier continues: "On passing Fort Asia, the sentinel hailed us, and desired us to land. Lord Byron, who had recovered his gaiety with the rising of the moon, swore, in good modern Greek, that he would not land to please any Turk in Asia; whereupon the sentinel thought proper to practise firing at a mark, and began at the boat; he did not hit us, and we were soon out of his reach, for the current swept us at about the rate of six knots, and we had a sail into the bargain.

"We arrived safe, although the crew nearly mutinied when the first shot was fired. They might as well have attempted to move the mosque of St. Sophia as turn Byron from his determination, which none but a woman could effect. It was a saying in after-life of Lord Byron's servant, 'Every woman can govern my lord—but my lady.' It appears by all accounts that men could neither intimidate nor manage the poet; he certainly was not easily led by our sex.

"At last the firman arrived, but the wind gradually died away, and the *Salsette* came to anchor once more close under the fort of Abydos. The next day Lord Byron was up early, and made arrangements for his second and more successful attempt at swimming the Hellespont. Mr. Ekenhead, an officer of marines, proposed to dispute the honour, and both gentlemen left the ship about nine o'clock, and landed on the European side. Above Sestos there is a narrow point of land which juts into the Dardanelles, and below Abydos there is a similar formation of coast, the point of the sandy bay on the Asiatic side projecting some distance. From point to point, that is, if they were opposite to each other, the distance would be about a mile—certainly not more; but as the current is rapid, and as it is impossible to swim directly across, the distance actually passed over would be between four or five miles.

"Mr. Ekenhead took the lead, and kept it the whole way. He was much the better swimmer of the two, and by far the more powerful man. He accomplished his task, according to Lord Byron's account, in an hour and five minutes, and his lordship at one and a quarter. Both were fresh and free from fatigue, especially Ekenhead, who did not leave the water until Lord Byron arrived."

Poor Ekenhead did not live to read the lines in *Don Juan* in which this feat is referred to. They are in the second canto (stanza cv.) where Juan's aquatic powers are described:

> He could, perhaps, have pass'd the Hellespont,
> As once (a feat on which ourselves we prided)
> Leander, Mr. Ekenhead and I did.

On hearing of his promotion to captain, when the *Salsette* eventually returned to Malta, Ekenhead managed to tumble over the bridge which then separated Nix Mangiare Stairs from Valetta, after a party in celebration, and was killed on the spot.

In Constantinople, when the ship at last reached that place, Chamier had many strange experiences, several of which he was again fortunate enough to share with Byron. Among them was a ceremonial visit to the Sultan, Mahmoud II, during which they partook of the usual protracted oriental feast, and were afterwards robed. They also witnessed the bowstringing of no fewer than forty men accused of piracy, and the beheading of their leader, whose body was publicly exposed.

"Byron looked with horror at the appalling scene," says Chamier. "No man can form an idea of the distorted sight who has not seen it; and neither am I very much inclined to recall to my recollection the horrible appearance of the corpse. Not far from this exhibition stood a melancholy-looking Turk, endeavouring to scare away some dogs; but his attempts were fruitless, for, unmindful of our presence, they rushed at the body, and began lapping the blood, which still oozed from the neck. I never remember to have shuddered with so cold a shudder as I did at that moment; and Byron, who ejaculated a sudden 'Good God!' turned abruptlyaway." It wasaltogetherascene never to be obliterated from a man's memory, and on a boy's mind it left the most unpleasant recollection. Those lines in the *Siege of Corinth* which few could ever scan with delight, are the vivid representation of the above anecdote:

> And he saw the lean dogs beneath the wall
> Hold o'er the dead their carnival;
> Gorging and growling o'er carcass and limb,
> They were too busy to bark at him.

The frigate remained in Constantinople no less than four months before Mr. Adair, the English minister, was ready to embark. When finally clear of the Hellespont, Bathurst directed his course towards the island of Zea, where they were to part with Byron. Chamier wrote: "It fell to my duty to land his lordship; and, in the discharge of this service, I had a warm and friendly shake of the hand from the first poet of the age, and received a handful of sequins to distribute to the boat's crew. Some Greeks took charge of his little luggage, for in this respect he was more slenderly provided than any traveller I ever knew. He turned towards the frigate, waved his handkerchief as an adieu, and then advanced into the interior of the island."

In summing up his boyish impression of the poet, Chamier says: "Every man who had the honour of Lord Byron's acquaintance, and who has since ventured before the public, has spoken much of his lordship's handsome appearance. As I consider beauty as only applicable to women, I would be understood here to attach the same weight to the word 'handsome' that is generally given to beauty. I shall not place my opinion at variance with those who knew him a hundred times better than myself; but certainly the impression on my mind is, that he was by no means the *very* handsome man some have imagined him to be.

"The deformity of limb, which annoyed him through

life, was conspicuous to any man with eyes in his head; and it was perfectly impossible for any shoemaker to disguise the clump foot. I really can scarcely credit that his lordship was so mortified at this visitation of Providence, when I have seen him thousands of times sitting on the taffrail, and swinging his legs about with unrestrained freedom. The fame which crowned his lordship in after-life made me anxious to remember his person and his manners, and I am quite satisfied that on board the *Salsette* he never took any particular pains to hide his feet. He certainly did not swim across the Hellespont in Hessian boots; and he dressed himself in the boat when he failed in his first attempt."

Chamier never afterwards chanced upon his romantic hero; but his impressions, as fresh as they were casual, have a charm which reflects as happily upon him as upon the poet.

II

Although Chamier was unlucky enough to miss Trafalgar, he served in the disastrous naval war of 1812 with America, during which his Admiral, Sir Peter Parker, was killed in his arms. He had, too, his fill of other excitement. Years later he met Bolivar. Besides these personal recollections, his work is full of the incidents of naval life, which even in peace time are often remarkable. Such, for instance, was the affair of the *Magpie* schooner. The time would have been somewhere between the years 1827 and 1831, when the ship was under the command of Lieutenant Smith, her duty being to cruise off Cuba, in the hope of intercepting a pirate vessel which had already caused much damage, and which was sending insurance rates sky-high. One evening, in the calm between the fall of the sea breeze and the coming of that from the land, the ship lay towards the shore and about eight miles away from the Colorados, a shoal at the western end of the island. Her fore-topsail was set, the yard braced for the starboard tack. On the port bow, a small dark cloud hung over the land; otherwise all appeared serene.

The cloud grew, and the mate, who was on watch, became at length a trifle anxious. "Mr. Smith," he called down, "I think the land breeze is coming off rather strong, sir; the clouds look very black."

"Very well," replied the captain; "keep a sharp look out. I shall be on deck myself in a moment."

Unfortunately, the mate did no more. Had he braced the fore-yard round, or furled the fore-topsail, the trouble might have been averted. He did neither, and a squall of wind, seeming to strike the vessel almost from alongside, instantly capsized her, almost before the watch had time to reach the deck.

The crew numbered twenty-four, of whom two were drowned at once. Then a calm set in, the moon shone brightly, and the ship's boat, though half full of water, floated with the survivors around her. But their unmethodical struggles merely rolled her over and over, and although all were safe from immediate death, unless and until the boat was righted, those who clung to her gunwales or scrambled on to her keel would certainly perish in time from exhaustion.

Smith, as soon as he could take command of the situation, ordered the boat to be righted, while two men got inside her to bale out the water with their hats. The others hung on to the gunwales until she was ready to receive fresh men for baling; and thus by degrees all could hope for rescue. Everything was going as well as the circumstances permitted until a man shouted that he saw the fin of a shark. Immediately there was panic, the boat was once more upset, and a vicious scramble for safety began, without method and without effect.

The man's alarm seemed to have been false. Smith persuaded those who clung to the gunwale to splash with their legs, and after furious efforts four men were again baling hard in the righted boat. Then, quite suddenly, about fifteen sharks came in amongst the men. The boat was overturned and the position worse than ever.

Despite the general terror, the sharks did not at first seem inclined to seize their prize. They swam amongst the men, playing in the water, almost rubbing against them. But at last the real attack began. A limb was seized, a head disappeared under the water and, having once tasted blood, the fish continued their savagery.

Even at this dreadful moment the captain kept his courage and made his men obey him. The boat was again righted and baling renewed. Smith cheered the men in from the stern, but, remitting his own splashing for a moment, had both legs severed above the knee. Two men at once dragged him into the stern sheets, but the boat heeled over and he disappeared into the sea.

The *Magpie* was over-set at eight o'clock. By nine there were two survivors sprawled on the keel of the boat. The rest had perished. The sharks seemed for the time satisfied, and the two at length righted the boat, and once more began the task of baling. After many further alarms from the sharks, who, returning, swam close, they at length had most of the water clear. They then sank into an exhausted sleep, one forward and the other aft, so fearful that they scarcely dared to move.

When the sun awoke the two sailors it was only to make them realize their desperate position. Heat, hunger, thirst, and isolation were before them. They had no oars, no mast, nothing but the bare planks and a sailor's knife apiece. Hour upon hour they lay becalmed. They prayed, they quarrelled, they swore, they sucked salt water, and they shuddered at the sight of a fin. And then at last they saw a sail. It was a brig, and she was steering exactly in their direction with a light breeze behind her.

Their joy was frenzied. They did everything in their power to attract her attention. Their eyes were never off the ship. They shouted. They held a jacket aloft—and then, just as the brig was approaching within distance of rescue, the whole fabric of their hopes was destroyed: she bore away about three points and began to make more sail.

All the loose thwarts had been lost in the night; nor could they move one of the fixed thwarts in order to paddle towards the ship. As a last throw, one of the sailors decided to swim towards rescue. He jumped into the water, kicking as vigorously as he could, and came at length within hailing distance. Even then he was not seen. The brig passed him, he was almost exhausted, when his final desperate leaps in the water attracted the attention of a man in the rigging of the vessel. She was hove to, a boat was lowered, and both seamen were saved.

The brig was American, and her captain at first suspected the two men of being pirates turned loose in a mastless boat. The actual tale seemed scarcely credible. They were landed at Havannah, whence they were conveyed to Port Royal by man-o'-war. There they were court martialled. When the facts were known, they were recommended for promotion, and both ended their active service as warrant officers: a happy epilogue to as swift a disaster as ever occurred at sea.

III

Chamier's other great meeting, that with Bolivar, occurred almost at the end of his time at sea. He was not impressed by the patriot's looks, and described him as "a thin, haggard, worn-out man in appearance, but very different in reality; he looked as unlike a great man, or one capable of great creation, as any I ever saw; he resembled a French postilion more than a warrior. When he addressed me, he never looked at my face; but occasionally cast a quick, scrutinizing glance, more indicative of cunning than open manliness of behaviour." But he recognized his stature, saw something of his work of liberation, and felt his natural skill in leadership.

After much adventuring in South America, Chamier retired young, and gave to writing the energy he had taken to sea. Besides his novels, *Ben Brace*, *Jack Adams*, and many others, he wrote a book of travels in France and Switzerland, having chanced to be in France at the time of the Revolution of 1848. He was also given the task of continuing James's *Naval History of Great Britain* down to the time at which he himself left the sea, and it is thus he is known to naval writers. He died in 1870, slipping into eternity almost unnoticed, having narrowly missed that greater skill or talent which makes Marryat so vital.

WILLIAM IV AS A MIDSHIPMAN

From a painting by West in the National Maritime Museum, Greenwich

17

KING WILLIAM IV

I

LOOKING backwards along the line of men and women who have occupied the throne of England, one sees a splendid diversity of creatures: saints, scholars, poets, sailors, soldiers, statesmen, wits, *bons vivants*, murderers, and at least four women of character. In death as in life, all have had their share of attention; all with one curious exception, King William IV.

The reason is simple. The English people have immense affection for the throne. As an institution, the throne has in times past survived the most extraordinary catastrophes: civil wars, usurpations, revolutions, abdications, and long and most merited unpopularity. For a century now past, affection has had its justification and reward, but it is seldom realized that in the 1830's books and cartoons were published which were of such monstrous offence towards the royal family as would to-day be unthinkable.

The fact about William IV is that he was a joke; one of the few consistent jokes in English history. Words like "bluff" and "hearty" and "well-meaning" spring to the memory about him from school text-books, but they miss the mark. That he was recognized as a joke in his lifetime is clear. Did not Mrs. Jordan, the actress for whom he conceived a very serious attachment when in the navy, play *The Humorous Lieutenant* to coincide with their liaison?

William's early life is obscure, but, though it does not compare in interest to the years subsequent to his accession, it was by no means dull. His father, George III, had to provide employment for a large family, and William, the third son, was sent into the navy, where he actually saw fighting under Rodney, being present at the battle of Cape St. Vincent—the first, 1780—and at the relief of Gibraltar. Subsequently he served in the West Indies with Nelson, whom he always warmly befriended.

It is generous to interpret William's belief in Nelson as showing an ability to judge character, but it must be remembered that, though very young, Nelson, when William served with him on the West India station, was his superior officer. Nevertheless, his affection for him was marked and genuine. He was present at Nelson's marriage, indeed he actually gave away the bride, and his belief in him is at least of a piece with his belief, many years later, in his niece, the young Victoria.

His career afloat was abruptly broken at one point, for, upon being given command of a small ship, and ordered to an unpopular North American station, he cheerfully sailed home again across the Atlantic in rank disobedience of orders, and in a dangerous season, because he did not wish to winter on the other side. George III's displeasure at William's proceeding was so severe that the young Prince was seldom afterwards independently employed. Indeed he soon retired from active service at sea, and seeking the seclusion of Bushey Park and the company of the generous and celebrated Mrs. Jordan, he proceeded to found a large family, which in later years he took pains to advance.

After the death of the Regent's daughter, Princess Charlotte, when William came within easy possibility of the throne, two other events of importance occurred. He was advanced in naval rank, eventually becoming Lord High Admiral, a post which he filled with the highest irregularity; and in 1818, in his fifty-fourth year, he married Adelaide, daughter of the Duke of Saxe-Meiningen. In the race for heirs with his brother, the Duke of Kent (who had married in the same year), he lost; the children of his lawful marriage died; while the Duke of Wellington, in the interests of economy, relieved him of his Admiralty position after he had held it a very short time, and he retired once more to the Rangership of Bushey.

Although Mrs. Jordan died in Paris, some years after the separation, in poor circumstances, it is affecting to read (the authority is a Miss Clitherow, a personal friend of the royal family), that Queen Adelaide, after William's death, chose as a memento from Windsor Castle a "picture from his own room of all the family. It was a singular picture, all the Fitz-Clarences grouped, and in the room Mrs. Jordan hanging a picture on the wall, the King's bust on a pedestal, and all strikingly alike. . . . It shows a delicacy of feeling to her King which was beautiful." She adds, "It was a picture better out of sight for his memory."

Adelaide was a good deal more generous than other royalties had been. One story relates that, on the question being raised of the reduction of Mrs. Jordan's allowance, the actress replied by enclosing in a letter a handbill bearing the legend: "No money returned after the rising of the curtain."

II

In 1830 died George IV, and he who had hitherto, despite his rank and marriage, lived in comparative obscurity, a sailor turned country gentleman, became King of England at the mature age of sixty-five and was so "excited at the exaltation" (wrote Greville) "that he nearly went mad, and distinguished himself by a thousand extravagances of language and conduct to the alarm or amusement of all." It is scarcely surprising. It is common experience that, however certainly good fortune may have been expected, its actuality *is* highly exciting; and the new King was an excitable person. "He is a good egg," it was said, "but a little cracked." Though in his conduct to Mrs. Jordan he may appear callous, he was never so much a "Prince of Blackguards," as Brougham called him, as a figure of fun, a Jack-in-the-Box.

He had no real training for kingship; no inherent dignity; an enormous flow of speech; a comical appearance—his head was "like a pineapple," said Greville—high spirits; a peppery temper; much irresponsibility; and a good deal of political prejudice which did not arise so much from thought as from habit. Although the Duke of Wellington, then the responsible minister, said of him at first: "If I had been able to deal with my late master as I do with my present I should have got on a deal better," this accommodation to business was largely the result of ignorance. Service at sea had taught William punctuality, which was indeed an asset, but this, and his affability, were his two most positive qualities. The rest was consternation and laughter.

At George IV's funeral he behaved like a sergeant-major, shouting, "Generals, generals, keep step, keep step! Admirals, keep step!" while "his first speech to the Council," says Greville, "was well enough given, but his burlesque character began even then to show itself. . . . He spoke of his (late) brother with all the semblance of feeling, and in a tone of voice properly softened and subdued, but just afterwards, when they gave him the pen to sign the declaration he said in his usual tone, 'This is a damned bad pen you have given me!'" It must have been an odd meeting all through for: "Mr. James Buller began to swear Privy Councillors in the name of 'King George IV—William I mean,' to the great diversion of the Council." The mistake was scarcely surprising, since the sovereigns of England had borne the name of George for a hundred and sixteen years continuously.

On July 20, 1830, he inspected the Coldstream Guards, "dressed (for the first time in his life) in a military uniform, and with a great pair of gold spurs half-way up his legs like a game-cock, although he was not to ride, for having chalk-stones in his hands he can't hold the reins." Later in the day "he must needs put on his plainer clothes and start on a ramble about the streets; alone, too. In Pall Mall he met Watson Taylor, and took his arm and went up St. James's Street. There he was soon followed by a mob making an uproar, and when he got near White's a woman came up and kissed him." This, though it disturbed his friends, did not upset him in the slightest. "Oh, never mind all this," he said. "When I have walked about a few times they will get used to it, and will take no notice." At a party a few days later he dismissed his guests thus: "Now, ladies and gentlemen, I wish you a goodnight. I will not detain you any longer from your amusements, and shall go to my own, which is to go to bed; so come along, my Queen!"

He sent his son George Fitzclarence post-haste from the dinner table one day to Boulogne to invite his brother-in-law, the King of Würtemberg, to stay in England. They had a royal time. Greville was scandalized because William insisted on "dropping" his guest at Grillons Hotel after the ceremony ("The King of England *dropping* another King at a tavern!"), while another provided more protracted astonishment. On July 25, 1830, he announced his intention of dining with the Duke of Wellington, but "in the morning he took the King of Würtemberg to Windsor, and just at the hour when the Duke was expecting him to dinner, he was driving through Hyde Park back from Windsor— three barouches and four, the horses dead knocked up, in front the two Kings, Jersey and somebody else, all covered with dust."

The meal itself must have been uproarious. The Kings proceeded to Apsley House arm in arm, the Duke following. When dinner was over William told the band to play the merriest waltz they knew, for the toast he was about to give was "The Queen of Würtemberg." He then—there were no women present—made a long speech upon connubial felicity. The band were next ordered to play, "See the Conquering Hero Comes," and he proceeded upon a tremendous encomium of the Duke of Wellington and his victories over the French. Suddenly remembering the presence of the French Ambassador, he hastened to explain that it was, of course, a different France he spoke of, not that of his friend the reigning King of France. He need not have been apprehensive, for the French Ambassador, "not understanding one word . . . kept darting from his seat to make his acknowledgments, while Esterhazy held him down by the tail of his coat, and the King stopped him with his hand outstretched, all with great difficulty." Greville adds, "It was very comical."

To the Freemasons, on their presenting an address, he is said to have made a reply which has gone down to history: "Gentlemen, if my love for you equalled my ignorance of everything concerning you, it would be boundless."

III

After early excitements, things grew gradually calmer, or perhaps people grew used to the unexpected. Greville notes in the following year: "The King lives a strange life at Brighton, with rag-tag and bobtail about him, and always open house. The Queen is a prude and will not let the ladies come *décolleté* to her parties. George IV, who liked ample expanses of that sort, would not let them be covered."

On February 22, 1831, he had a nasty experience, for upon returning from the play he was "hooted and pelted" (the Reform Bill agitation was at its height) and a stone shivered a window of his coach and fell into Prince George of Cumberland's lap. The King was excessively annoyed and sent for the officer riding by his coach, and asked him if he knew who had thrown the stone. He said that it terrified the Queen, and "was very disagreeable, as he should always be going somewhere."

He next created a precedent by wearing mourning for his son-in-law Kennedy; danced a country dance with Lord Amelius Beauclerk, an old Admiral, at an evening party; crowned himself, improperly, in the robing room of the House of Lords; and when the ceremonial plans for the formal coronation were laid before him, refused to submit to being kissed by the Bishops, though he afterwards "knocked under." At a quiet dinner held soon afterwards at St. James's he made two speeches; the first, on "the land we live in," was delivered before the ladies left the room. The second, after they had gone, was in French, "in the course of which he travelled over every variety of topic which suggested itself to his excursive mind, and ended with a coarse toast and the words: *Honi soit qui mal y pense*"— all this, despite Miss Clitherow's grave assertion that "the King is two years older since he wore the crown."

Miss Clitherow gives an intimate glimpse of him in April 1831. After a private dinner which she had attended: "He unlocked a box, and set to work signing. . . . Three times he was obliged to stop, and put his hand in hot water, he had the cramp so severe in his fingers. When he signed the last he exclaimed, 'Thank God, 'tis done!' He looked at me and said, 'My dear madame, when I began signing I had forty-eight thousand signatures my poor brother should have signed. I did them all, but I made a determination never to lay my head on the pillow till I had signed everything I ought on the day, cost me what it might. It is cruel suffering, but, thank God! 'tis only cramp; my health never was better."

Two years later, his state appeared more alarming: "not," says Greville, "amounting to actual derangement, only morbid irritability and activity—reviewing the Guards and

blowing up people at court. . . . He had a musket brought
to him, that he might show them—the Guards—the way
to use it in some new sort of exercise he wanted to introduce;
in short, he gave a great deal of trouble and made a fool
of himself." At an art exhibition, on a picture of Admiral
Napier being shown to him—with whose politics he did
not then agree—Raikes reports him to have said to the
President who was showing him round, "Admiral Napier
be damned, sir! And may you be damned, sir! And if the
Queen were not here, sir, I would kick you downstairs, sir!"

The Duke of Wellington had a bothersome time with
him in 1835, for he was full of whims. In one letter he
begged "to call the attention of the Duke to the *theoretical*
state of Persia"; in another, urged him to consent to war
with China; and in another, expressed a wish to buy the
Island of St. Bartholomew, lest the Russians should get it.
"He is," adds Greville, "very jealous of Russia."

IV

In 1835 Adolphus Fitzclarence, the King's third son,
gave Greville an intimate picture of his father's way of life.
"He sleeps in the same room with the Queen, but in a separate
bed; at a quarter before eight every morning his *valet de
chambre* knocks at the door, and at ten minutes before
eight exactly he gets out of bed, puts on a flannel dressing-
gown and trousers, and walks into his dressing-room. . . .
He is long at his ablutions, and takes up an hour and a half
in dressing. At half-past nine he breakfasts with the Queen,
the ladies, and any of his family; he eats a couple of fingers
and drinks a dish of coffee. At breakfast he reads *The Times*
and *Morning Post*, commenting aloud on what he reads in
very plain terms, and sometimes they hear, 'That's a damned
lie,' or some such remark, without knowing to what it
applies. After breakfast he devotes himself to business till

two, when he lunches (two cutlets and two glasses of sherry); then he goes out for a drive till dinner-time; at dinner he drinks a bottle of sherry—no other wine—and eats moderately; he goes to bed soon after eleven."

His speechifying and general eccentricity continued, though for the most part he was in lower spirits and was fast ageing. It was in this year, 1835, that his animadversion towards the Duchess of Kent began, which ended in one of the most astounding scenes in the royal family history. The Duchess had been conducting a series of pompous progresses all over the country with her daughter Victoria, now heiress to the Crown; guns had popped in salute so incessantly that William became severely annoyed, speaking openly of his "respect" for the young Victoria, an odd adjective (if just) to use of a child, and of his distrust of "the persons by whom she is surrounded."

In the following year, 1836, the storm burst. The King asked the Duchess to go to Windsor to celebrate the Queen's birthday, on August 13th, and also his own, on August 21st. The Duchess refused the first invitation, but said she would arrive at Windsor on the 20th. The King was furious, but made no reply, and on August 20th, being in London for the prorogation of Parliament, he proceeded to Kensington Palace where "he found that the Duchess of Kent had appropriated for her own use a suite of apartments, seventeen in number, for which she had applied last year, and which he had refused to let her have." Arriving at Windsor he voiced his displeasure in public, and the next day, in a speech at his birthday dinner, gave the Duchess one of the most terrific harangues he had ever, even in a reign of speechifying, composed.

"This awful philippic," says Greville, "was uttered in a loud voice and excited manner. The Queen looked in deep distress, the Princess burst into tears, and the whole company were aghast. . . . Immediately after they rose and retired, and a terrible scene ensued; the Duchess announced her immediate departure and ordered her carriage, but a sort of reconciliation was patched up, and she was prevailed upon to stay till the next day."

That was the last firework. The sequel occurred in the year following when William, aged and ill, offered the young Victoria £10,000 a year from his Privy Purse, a charming gesture. The Duchess, of course, disputed the arrangement of payment, but the matter was never settled, for on June 20, 1837, the King died, and the long reign of Victoria began.

On the whole William died regretted. He had been a fresh sea-breeze; and if he provoked laughter it was difficult not to like him. He was as different a man from his brother as could be conceived, and his odd personality possibly saved the monarchy, or at least tided it over a few difficult years, for if the purely personal side of William IV's reign, with which this sketch is concerned, was in the nature of a comic interlude, an ironic commentary is provided by the political background. At the outset William found himself in a mess—that of the Reform Bill. That he bore at his death the grandiloquent title of the "Reform Monarch of England" was scarcely more than another comicality. Reform was thrust upon him ("Who is Silly Billy now!" unjustly exclaimed his brother of Gloucester when the Act was signed); and he countenanced the government of the successful Whig Ministers with what was often irritation. It was perhaps fortunate that this was the one and only severe national crisis of his short reign.

18

GENERAL DYOTT

Most of us have in our mind's eye a pattern of perfection for at least one or two aspects of life. We see, for instance, the apotheosis of the Highland chief in Raeburn's portrait of Sir John Sinclair; we see the hero revealed through Nelson's letters, and the administrator's through St. Vincent's. We see the perfect diarist in Pepys, enhanced, if that is possible, by Hayls's humorous rendering of his features; the naturalist in Gilbert White; the Christian pastor in George Herbert; the wit in Marvell; the humorist in Lamb. These are types beyond which it is scarcely possible to go; they set a standard in their kind.

To those lucky enough to have read the two volumes of Dyott's *Diary* will have been unfolded a picture of the traditional Englishman in his hey-day, conservative to the core, with the frankness and ability to reveal himself steadily on paper over the span of sixty-four years. Possibly this is a record length for a diary of any consequence. Dyott lived from 1761–1847. He started with an entry in 1781: "Journal; no, it is not a journal; well, what you please, Mr. William." He ended three years before his death. Between the two dates he painted a self-portrait whose colour glows freshly across the years; one full of vigour, charm and human imperfection.

William Dyott, to those who chance upon him, is very nearly too good to be true. He conforms so perfectly to idea—like the half-fictitious, though wholly convincing, Sir Roger de Coverley of an earlier time—that as his pages grow and the man slowly spreads himself, not startlingly, not by the memorable phrase or paragraph, but with detail and precision, it becomes overwhelmingly clear that the legend of the "fine old English gentleman" had more than a literary reality. Dyott, who never wrote for effect, never afterwards looked at what he wrote, and never penned a false sentence, displays the substance behind the phrase.

He came of a Staffordshire family, one of whose members, though deaf and dumb, killed the Parliamentarian, Lord Brooke, in his attack on Lichfield in the Civil War. He chose the army as his profession, and (having purse) rose with much rapidity. By 1794, at the age of thirty-three, he was a major. Seven years later he was a brigadier, and A.D.C. to King George III, a monarch for whom he had the staunchest admiration. Nor, although he missed the hard campaigns of the time in India and Spain, as well as Waterloo, was he merely a parade-ground man. He went to Nova Scotia in 1787, where he made the acquaintance and enjoyed almost the friendship of Prince William, afterwards William IV, a post-captain in the navy, and then, as always, alarmingly eccentric. He saw active service in the West Indies in 1796 during the capture of Grenada; fought against insurgents supported by the French; was under Ludlow at Alexandria in 1801; narrowly missed joining Sir John Moore's staff in Spain through the death of the commander and the withdrawal of his army, and was in the disastrous Walcheren Expedition of 1809. That was the sum of his campaigning, crowned by an appointment as lieutenant-general in 1813.

Dyott may be said to have been lucky. He missed the fame of service under Wellington, yet endured the whistle of hostile bullets, and knew the sterner side of the soldier's calling. He saw much of the world, made a vast acquaintance, particularly among the peerage, and when he retired he could look back upon a strenuous and successful career. Moreover, there is no doubt he was a good officer. He wrote without hesitation of the low type to be found in the ranks in his time, and he supported the brutality of flogging long after it had become apparent that it was a stupid and antique punishment. But there is no single entry in the whole course of his service on the active list which gives ground for thinking him anything but paternal as well as efficient: whilst in the Walcheren campaign his concern over the conditions of his sick is manifest. Dyott was a disciplinarian: he was not a martinet.

So far, so good. Dyott had friends, rude health, sufficient money, a full life behind him and a pleasant prospect to come. But it is seldom that a man's affairs run perfectly—it would be dull if they always did. It was his wife who provided the one great failure of his long life. She ran away. Probably she fell in love; possibly Dyott bored her. Again, she may have been overwrought by the peregrinations and upsets of military life. But despite all his efforts to stay her, he could not, and she caused him to go through all the then cumbersome processes of a parliamentary divorce. Even so, the General may have been fortunate, for he was autocratic and obstinate, and the wives of his kinsmen and friends did not always please him, to say nothing of a queer spinster relation, Miss Bakwell, who haunted his house and pages, and whom he thoroughly disliked. Moreover, an extant portrait of Mrs. Dyott seems to indicate an almost sinister lack of mental qualities. She had practically no forehead; she was constantly ill; and if she left her husband for another, she bequeathed to his care three children—Dick Bill, and Eleanor—upon whom, to the day of his death, he lavished a wealth of affection and concern which they seem to have returned. Bill, it is true, had a lapse at Cambridge, where he wasted his time and ran up debts in the fashion of the day. But even in this respect he was only following in the footsteps of other young men who have afterwards turned themselves, as he did, into adequate clergymen.

Dyott is so candid about one of his less pleasing character-istics that, in the calm of the diary at any rate, it becomes almost exciting. He pulled strings. He pulled them with a tireless persistence which must, for various victims, have been a great nuisance. His own elevation had, it might have seemed, been quick enough, and indeed Dyott's efforts on his own behalf usually matured with small trouble. But when he retired he desired a colonelcy, and he plagued the War Office to such effect that, although he had to wait some years, he was eventually appointed to the 63rd Regiment, and promotion to full general came five years later. Afterwards there was Dick, his beloved heir, to consider. Dick was a model son, and evidently a charming character. He, too, took the army as his career. He would have liked to combine this with membership of Parliament in the Tory interest during his father's lifetime. He did not succeed, and his promotion in the army seemed to lack the expected speed. It is allowable to suspect that the General's continual badgering of Lord Hill and other notabilities had something to do with it. Seldom did he go to London but he was found in ante-rooms with the same request on his lips. It was monstrous, he inferred, that a general officer of his standing should have to offer to purchase the earlier steps for his son. The authorities must do something about it.

With his other son, Bill, he had better luck. Dyott was near neighbour in Staffordshire to Sir Robert Peel, which brought him, fortuitously, into constant intimacy with that great man. When Bill at last turned over a new leaf, took his degree and was ordained, it was not long before Dyott was able, through Peel's good offices, to get him a living. To this was added the appointment of a chaplaincy to Lord Combermere, which allowed Bill to top his vestments with a scarlet scarf. The General fondly looked forward to a second living for him "if it should offer." As for Eleanor, his dear daughter, who came to mean so much more to Dyott than ever his wife could have done, there was nothing—not even a trip to France in his old age, or countless jaunts to a London which, in its new growth, he came to dislike, and to courts which, he thought, made poor showing against those of George III—nothing he would not undergo for her amusement. The reader feels that she may marry and leave him: but there is never a hint of this happening in Dyott's lifetime. It was the one direction in which the General pulled no strings.

One of the delights of the greater diarists is that they enable the reader to peep over a shoulder, to look upon matter which he may or may not be meant to see. This is pre-eminently so with Pepys, and, if no other comparison is possible between Dyott and the great Secretary to the Admiralty, they at least had this in common: they were both intensely alive—alive to themselves as well as to the world—and they lived in supremely interesting times. Pepys watched the transformation of England in perhaps the most difficult years of her political evolution, his viewpoint including Court and City. Dyott, enjoying almost as many exalted friendships, his span in years far wider, saw the beginning of modern times. He did not like them.

Although as a boy Dyott had seen Dr. Johnson at Lichfield, it would have been as a Tory rather than as a sage that he would have valued him. He read little, and what he learned came rather from contact with his fellows than from books. He was thick with prejudice; so ardent an upholder of the *status quo*, from which he reaped so much, that his references to the "lower orders," and even to those "good worthy men" not quite of his own standing, seem to remove them into a different order of being. Helots they were, and such they should remain. New ideas horrified him. A radical (even if he happened to be a Marquess, a general officer, and a familiar friend, like Anglesea) was almost unspeakable. Even his early acquaintance with William IV could not curb the acidity of his remarks when he came to the throne and became involved in the tussle for parliamentary reform. He was apt then to remember the lack of restraint of His

Majesty's youth rather than his "condescension" to a humble officer of a line regiment.

Hidebound as he was in his political ideas, there was indeed one respect in which Dyott was open to change. He never looked at a field or a farm without keeping both eyes wide open for improvements at his own Freeford. It was a trait which lasted from youth until, in his old age, he introduced a new Scottish plough to his Midland ploughmen, and made them use it properly. Other things he came to accept, though grudgingly; among them, the steamer and the railway; but of the income tax which his friend Peel introduced he wrote, "As might be expected, it was strongly opposed in the House of Commons, and not very well received in the country."

With increasing years he became deaf, and, it might be added, rather self-conscious. He records more than once that he hopes his now swelling array of diaries may entertain his children after he is gone, and even that they may "venerate" his memory.

His deafness creeps more and more into prominence, though his general health remained magnificent, as he records in an interview with a celebrated Leamington practitioner, Dr. Jephson. "I called upon him," he writes, "and after he had gone through the regular routine of squeezing the wrist and beholding the tongue, he said, 'All I have to prescribe is, consult no doctors; there is not a man in England of your age in better health.' (Dyott was seventy-seven.) My acknowledgment was, 'I conclude, as you don't write me a prescription, I may keep the fee in my pocket.' 'Certainly,' replied the doctor."

That is the General to the life. So is the incident he records which took place in a Birmingham shop. He advanced, after making a purchase, saw a man in front coming towards him, and stepped aside to let him pass. The stranger did the same. Dyott made a courtly bow, and the man did the like. Dyott then peered at the figure closer, to find that it was himself reflected in a glass. This story had wide currency, but here, one feels, is the original.

Towards the last he grew aware of having become a "character." Increasingly he refers to himself as "the Old General," and the reader is made to feel the difficulties, either as host or guest, of accommodating the deaf. But everyone remains kind and attentive; Dyott saves money, and adds to his cherished ancestral property at Freeford. Although he broke off his diary before the end came, his luck held. He died at eighty-six, his children around his bedside.

England, even his own Staffordshire, has given birth to many more distinguished soldiers than General William Dyott, but none whom we can know so closely. For the strangest part about the diary is that, although it is immensely long, and has no purely literary distinction or grace, it stays vivid to the last page. The final entry is, "On the 3rd of April, began sowing barley."

19

THE PERSONAL TOUCH
AT BALACLAVA

I

IF ever it had much justification, it is good to believe that the invidious distinction made by an old encyclopaedia between Intelligence (Military) and Intelligence (General) is no more. "It is a comfort to find," wrote a young officer on active service in modern times, "that the new army thinks less and less about tigers and more and more about the symphonies of Sibelius." That may be an exaggeration; yet there was a time—not very remote either—when the curve and sweep of the white moustache, eminently military, was an emblem of boldness without brain, and the adornment has been displayed with a fine generosity in the English-speaking world for many a decade.

The fierce moustache has illuminated so many advertisements—never slow to filch the fun from satire—that its owners as a race have come to have an existence strong in their own right. So much is this true, that a victim of this mass assault may be pardoned for his delight in finding what must surely be the fount and origin of the very idea; in his rediscovery of prototypes in life whose story seems almost too good to be believed. But it is true they lived, and some of the purest specimens are displayed in the pages of a collector no less eminent than Kinglake.

It is, indeed, necessary to go back as far as the Crimea to discover the full gloss of the moustache. The heroes of still earlier wars do not fit the picture—young men on gaunt hunters, reconnoitring before Salamanca: these will not do. But the cavalry in the Crimea was led at first by aristocratic

162

old generals who conform perfectly to pattern. By their acts ye shall know them, and never were men more lavish in giving knowledge of themselves to their fellows. Nor have they been forgotten. Echoes of the dunder-headed war in which they took part can yet be found on the walls of many a tavern; in current street names; in Tennyson; and in the background of popular books and films. For instance, it is the horror of the white moustache which haunts the early years of the hero of *The Four Feathers*.

"I don't know what they'll do to the enemy, but, by God! they frighten me." Such indeed must be the general verdict on, for instance, the explosive heroes of the most famous cavalry incident of its age—the charge of the Light Brigade at Balaclava. So perfectly does Balaclava illustrate the spirit of the white moustache that it is worth recalling the main people involved in that tremendous episode. One of the commanders, Lord Lucan—the whole affair bristles with the peerage—is still remembered by a very few. For instance, Lord Midleton in his old age gave us a fascinating glimpse of Lucan in his. He was a man of whom a hostess once said that she was amazed anyone could choose to go to a play when they could see Lord Lucan. Lord Cardigan was in his way as good. Between them they contrived that the din of controversy should be as deafening as that of war.

II

The battle itself was a proper botch. Kinglake describes from first-hand evidence, and with lingering detail, the springs of failure. There was age: Lucan, the senior cavalry officer, was fifty-four and had seen little service, none in a British command; Cardigan, fifty-seven, was purely a Hyde Park soldier, a rule-of-thumb commander of the most rigid kind, though devoted to his profession. There was temper. There was money, since Cardigan had risen by "purchase, and by favour of the Duke of York." Lucan, too, had been able to buy pretty steady rises in rank, though he had never rivalled in largesse the £10,000 a year Cardigan was reputed to lavish on his regiment, the 11th Hussars. His Lancers, the 17th, were, however, known for a time as Bingham's Dandies—Bingham being his family name. Lastly, though it did not affect the issue, there was personal relationship. The two earls were brothers-in-law; none the better friends for that. The clubs had teetered when they heard of their close conjunction, and expected sparks to fly. Never could they have hoped for such a dazzling display as was actually provided. Unlike most fireworks, these went on.

More remarkable characters, within their particular type, could not easily be conceived. Lucan, says Kinglake, "enjoyed perfect health; he saw like a hawk;" he was "tall, lithe, slender," and he pursued his business

with a kind of fierce, tearing energy. . . . At every fresh access of strenuousness, and especially at the moments expressing strenuous speech, his face all at once used to light up with a glittering, panther-like aspect, resulting from the sudden fire of the eye, and the sudden disclosure of the teeth, white, even and clenched.

Hitherto, his immense energies had been directed upon "large agricultural operations," his troops, his Irish and English tenantry. His intelligence, like his temper, was of a highly positive kind.

Lord Cardigan, gifted with a share of his family's good looks, had a passion for detail, was a martinet, and a great lover of himself. Like Lucan, he was not a popular officer, and his temper had already led him into copious trouble. "One of his quarrels," recalls Kinglake, "was founded upon the colour of a bottle; another upon the size of a tea-cup." In personal habits, the Generals were in strong contrast. Lucan lived under canvas; Cardigan had a luxurious yacht off Balaclava harbour, and not only slept there, but had a French cook. Lucan possessed most of the Spartan virtues;

Cardigan's private life was lurid. The courage of both men was unimpeachable. Such were the two soldiers entrusted with leading cavalry in a situation of crisis. Lucan held divisional command; Cardigan had the Light Brigade; while a third General, Scarlett, a brigadier as enterprising as he was eager to profit from experience, led the Heavy Brigade, and ultimately took Lucan's place.

Two other personalities remain to be considered. Field-Marshal Lord Raglan, the Commander-in-Chief, was King-lake's hero. He had lost an arm serving on Wellington's staff in the Peninsula, and was a man who commanded devotion and obedience. Among his aides-de-camp was Nolan, a captain of cavalry, passionate in his belief in the supremacy of mounted men. Lucan and Cardigan, neither of whom took orders from headquarters with the best grace, seem to have shared a particular distrust of Nolan, who, misguided man, had written a book. It was about cavalry, but still a book.

III

The tactical details of Balaclava belong to history; the part of the Light Brigade to verse. It is in asides that the interest of the day remains vivid. To Lucan, it was the first true test of leadership, since the cavalry had played no leading part in earlier encounters. It cannot be said that in the opening stages of the fight he had shown verve. Most of the credit of the successful charge of the Heavy Brigade belongs to Scarlett, and to the consistent passivity of the Russian horse, who allowed themselves to be routed uphill, and from the halt. The Light Brigade, under Cardigan, at first looked on; and when they were at last called into action, wrong-headedness, lack of visibility from his post, and—as he thought—the impertinent way in which Nolan delivered Lord Raglan's orders to advance, sent the Light

Brigade into the valley of death. They rode to destruction against positions other than were intended, enfiladed, and full in the face of Russian cannon.

Both Lucan and Cardigan conducted the operation passionate against Nolan, not the Russians: Lucan for the aide's seeming aspersion on his whole handling of the cavalry; Cardigan because Nolan, seeing that the Light Brigade was taking the wrong direction, dashed across its front waving a directive sword. Before he could explain himself further to the brigadier a shell splinter pierced his heart. His horse turned, and Nolan, giving a shriek which struck all who heard it cold, fell dead among the advancing troopers.

Cardigan led the Brigade in person, and "like a gentleman." Those were the words of an officer near him: Kinglake says to perfection. He steadied it, actually keeping back with the flat of his sword a man who pressed too fast, while subordinate officers continued to "dress" the lines of men. Shot and shell moved him not at all, and he was first in among the Russian guns, receiving a slight leg wound. But there virtue deserted him; for he made no attempt to find or to rally his shattered squadrons, and he rode slowly back the way he had come, leaving the glory of leading the actual encounter with the Russians to Lord George Paget, son of a peer who had himself led a famous charge at Waterloo.

Cardigan's first remark upon returning was to blast Nolan for trying to lead his Brigade, and for "shrieking like a woman." He had almost ridden over his dead body, though he did not know it. "It is a mad-brained trick," he said, when the remnants of his shattered force paraded before him, "but it is no fault of mine." The soldiers, with imperturbable cheerfulness, answered, "Never mind, my lord! we are ready to go again." Of nearly seven hundred men, not two hundred answered the roll-call.

Lord Raglan had seen the whole disaster from an eminence commanding the battle-field. First reprimanding Cardigan, he then met Lord Lucan, and said, with a voice of reproach and anger, "You have lost the Light Brigade." It was true enough, though Lucan, and all concerned with the deed, had won immortality.

IV

If "someone had blundered," as Tennyson said, and if it had rested at that, the Legend of the White Moustache might have found a later origin. But blunders breed inquiries; in this instance prolifically. Nolan lay dead on the field, but the two peers remained not merely alive but vocal. They returned to England. Lucan was officially recalled, and Cardigan, his command destroyed, got himself invalided. Soon the clubs buzzed not only with the exploit, but with argument. This, in the decades which followed, grew stale beyond imagination. It would perhaps have been better if Lucan had been granted the court martial he desired. The blame would then have come home to at least an official roost.

As might have been guessed, Cardigan's voice was the most persistent, if not the loudest. He sang his own praises after a City banquet in a way which brought a deeper hue to the ruddiest countenance. He litigated; he justified; he poured memoranda on the patient Kinglake, and at last he died, having alienated the sympathy of the men he led, and having, among later exploits, rushed from the death-bed of his wife to the arms of his mistress, saying—in her own version—that "now they could be married at once."

Lucan, who lived to the good age of eighty-eight, remained a thunderer to the last. The House of Lords as well as the clubs had long grown weary of the whole business when, in 1887, they made him a Field-Marshal. At a dinner in celebration of the event he electrified the whole assembly, including the Duke of Cambridge—who had himself been present at Balaclava—by complaining that they had given his Quartermaster-General the same honour years before, and that it was none too soon that they paid him a like respect.

Time has drawn a kindly veil over these personal repercussions, leaving the memory of the Charge itself undimmed. But it is indeed a double-edged blessing for the white moustache when its glories survive a stricken field. Postmortems on a game of bridge are as thistledown by comparison with those on "battles long ago," and there are occasions when, for the sake of reputation, gold is as dross against the worth of silence. The white moustache is in itself a noble object; all the nobler if it is never waggled in unseemly argument.

20

HICKS PASHA

I

WHEN senior officers retire, it is usually to honourable obscurity. It is given to few to achieve, at the age of over fifty, a really decisive misfortune, one which in its outcome adds a country to an empire. This was the fate of William Hicks, better known as Hicks Pasha, leader of a famous and ill-fated expedition to the Sudan.

Until his emergence, comparatively late in life, as leader of the first large expedition against the Mahdi, Hicks's career, if one of merit, was without particular eminence. Joining the Bombay army as an ensign in 1849, at the age of nineteen, he served as a lieutenant with the first Belûchî Battalion in the campaign of 1857–59; as a staff officer in the Punjab mobile column; and in the Rohikland campaign under Lord Clyde. In 1861 he was given his company. He served in the Abyssinian campaign as brigade-major in the 1st Division; was promoted lieutenant-colonel in 1875, and retired five years later with the rank of honorary colonel, his military life to all appearances being over.

When the Mahdi first appeared as a religious leader in the Sudan, few of those in authority could foresee the immense political consequences which his uprising would bring about, or the power of his following. It was thought in Egypt that a single expedition of moderate force, capably led, would suffice to annihilate what military power he possessed. This the Government in Cairo resolved to send, and, on the recommendation of Valentine Baker Pasha, then commanding the Egyptian Gendarmerie, Colonel Hicks was offered, and accepted, the post of command.

On February 7, 1883, Hicks left Cairo with a European staff. The party reached the Nile port of Berber by a march across the desert from the Red Sea town of Suâkin, a journey graphically described by Colonel Colborne, an officer who was later invalided home. From Berber, the staff proceeded down the Nile to Khartoum, where Hicks joined his army.

Mr. Churchill has described Hicks's force as being "perhaps the worst army that has ever marched to war." This is a statement which needs modification, although at no time were the existing military authorities in Khartoum confident of its qualities. Many of those who comprised it had but recently suffered defeat, with their leader, Arabi Pasha, at Tel-el-Kebir, from Wolseley's British force, and their first few manoeuvres under Hicks's command filled him with fury and dismay. Nevertheless, Colonel Colborne spoke highly of the conduct of the five thousand men who, with four Nordenfeldt guns, advanced from Khartoum into the province of Sennar to subjugate revolt in the country between the Blue and the White Nile. An early reconnaissance by Colborne up the White Nile to Kawa had disclosed the presence of a considerable number of the enemy, and, on April 29th, a battle was fought at Marabia in which about four thousand Dervishes were severely defeated by the Egyptians, who fought steadily and kept their square unbroken, despite the reckless charges of the enemy.

Losses to the Government troops were few, while those to the enemy were considerable and included several notable sheikhs. Colborne, who himself thought highly not only of his own men but of the enemy, records that many of the Arabs fought in mail armour, and that, although for the most part unarmed with rifles, they did not consider it chivalrous to attack except in the open. The result, disastrous to themselves, provided a lesson in tactics which they very readily learned.

Having secured this small success, Hicks and his troops returned to Khartoum, leaving the province of Sennar, as they thought, quieted and secure. This security was an illusion, and from the time of Marabia Hicks's troubles may be said to have begun.

The influence of the Mahdi, particularly in that part of the Sudan into which the advance had been made, the Gezira, and also to the west, in Kordofan and Darfur, was increasing daily. The fanatical zeal of his followers was tremendous, as was their hatred of the Egyptians, who nominally governed but actually oppressed the country. More important still, the fall of such towns as Bara and El Obeid had placed him in possession of many rifles; nor was he slow to see that his men were instructed in their use. There were, moreover, many regulars and irregulars, formerly in the service of the Government, now enrolled under the Mahdi's banner. His men, besides religious zeal and genuine political wrongs, had victories as well as defeats to remember, while it was becoming known that the condition of Hicks's force was deteriorating, and that the disposition of some of its Egyptian officers towards the European staff was far from cordial. To add to Hicks's troubles, the Egyptian Treasury was virtually bankrupt, and some of his men were months in arrears of pay.

Nor was the position eased by the great distance of Hicks's headquarters from the seat of Government at Cairo; by the attitude of strict non-interference with the affairs of the Sudan maintained by the Government of Great Britain; or by the fact that the Khedive thought fit to send Ala-el-Din Pasha to Khartoum in the capacity of Governor-General of the Sudan. Indeed the situation became so intolerable that Hicks threatened resignation, and a crisis was only averted by his appointment as General of Division and Commander-in-Chief.

As reports of the Mahdi's successes against the Egyptian

garrisons continued, it was now decided to send an expedition of 10,000 men to attempt the subjugation of Kordofan. It was a plan which was made against the judgment of every responsible authority in Khartoum. Time was not of immediate consequence, while the effects of a possible failure would, it was realized, be of the utmost gravity. Hicks was prepared to attempt the campaign with the force suggested (which was already assembled in Khartoum), and with the full knowledge that a defeat, in his own words, "might mean not only the loss of Darfur and Kordofan, but also of Sennar and possibly Khartoum." In Lord Cromer's opinion Hicks's expression of willingness to accede to the plan at all was caused by "the reluctance naturally felt by a gallant soldier to appear to shrink from a dangerous undertaking." It is difficult to believe that Hicks understood precisely how slender were his chances.

II

On September 9, 1883, the General and his army left Omdurman. His force, actually less than 10,000, consisted of 7,000 infantry, 400 mounted Bashi-Bazooks, 500 cavalry, 100 Circassians, 10 mountain guns, 4 Krupp guns, and 6 Nordenfeldt machine guns. It was a miscellaneous assembly indeed, with a small though able European staff of about ten officers, English and German, and it was hampered by the presence of Ala-el-Din Pasha himself, who "exercised an uncertain authority." The pitiful condition of some of the units is best conveyed by Hicks's own words in a letter to Sir Evelyn Wood. "Fifty-one men of the Krupp battery deserted on the way here [to Khartoum] *although in chains*."

It can have happened but seldom that an expedition has set out with such a foreboding of doom. The European and Egyptian officers remained throughout on bad terms, their one point of unity, according to a deserter, being a complete lack of confidence in victory. Wild stories were circulated of the relations between Hicks and Ala-el-Din Pasha, and of the straits to which Hicks was reduced in order to maintain his command.

The army ascended the White Nile as far as Duem, accompanied by an unofficial rear-guard of numbers of Arabs, whose disposition was always doubtful. At Duem, it struck across the desert.

Why this decision was made remains obscure. The army was entering what was well known to be one of the driest and hottest parts of the Sudan. The water supply was likely to be uncertain; guides were unreliable and were as often as not spies; and Hicks, rightly or wrongly, decided to leave his rear unprotected, as he considered that the maintenance of a series of posts would too seriously weaken his force. His aim was El Obeid, recently fallen into the hands of the Mahdi. The more obvious route would have been by the northerly road through Gebra and Bara, which had the advantage of covering open ground and of a small, though assured, supply of water in certain places. Slatin Pasha relates that at Duem, on someone asking Hicks what he thought of the situation, he replied quietly, "I am like Jesus Christ in the midst of the Jews." "Still he marched on," adds Slatin. "Perhaps he thought that if he refused to advance, his honour might be impugned."

The appearance of the force must have been astonishing. Slatin received accounts from eyewitnesses and survivors, which he records as follows:

Ten thousand men, in square formation, with six thousand camels in their midst, were to march through districts overgrown with vegetation and grass taller than a man's height. . . . They must be ready at any moment for the attack of an enemy far more numerous and as well armed as themselves. . . . Six thousand camels, huddled together in the centre of a square, presented a perfect forest of heads and necks; it was impossible for a bullet fired by one of the enemy from behind a tree to miss altogether this gigantic target; if it failed to strike in front, it would almost certainly have its billet in the centre or rear.

Slowly the huge, despondent mass toiled on, leaving a trail of dead and dying animals; short of water; sometimes harassed by isolated bodies of the enemy; daily moving farther from the Nile and into unknown country. When first the westward advance into the desert began, O'Donovan, a newspaper correspondent who, with an artist named Vizetelly, was attached to the force, wrote: "We shall be shut off from the outer world for a time." It was his last letter home. Colonel Farquhar, the chief of staff, one day asked O'Donovan where he thought the army would be eight days hence. "In Kingdom Come," was the reply. Not many days later, his German servant, Klootz, deserted to the enemy, convinced of the hopelessness of the issue. The Mahdi asked him if he thought there was the least chance of Hicks's surrender. Klootz shook his head. O'Donovan's entry in his journal relating to Klootz reads as follows: "What must be the condition of an army when even a European servant deserts to the enemy?"

The force slowly made its way through Shatt and Rahad, and on the approach of the Government troops, the Mahdi himself marched out of El Obeid to prepare for battle. More than 50,000 men assembled in his camp, while he himself, taking up a position beneath an enormous Adansonia tree near the town, confidently awaited Hicks's advance. He employed his men in military exercises, and at the same time issued hundreds of summonses calling upon the English officers to surrender. These were, of course, unanswered.

Before leaving Duem, Hicks had been informed by the Government that he would be joined *en route* by 6,000 men from Jebel Tagalla. None came, nor did he receive a word of news. On leaving Rahad he advanced to Aluba in the hope of obtaining a good supply of water; and, on November 3rd, he reached Kashgil, a place about thirty miles south-east of El Obeid.

On that day, according to all accounts, the Mahdi's real

attack began. It was well chosen. The dispirited troops were already beginning to suffer the tortures of thirst. Their camels were for the most part exhausted, and were dying by scores; and they were still a considerable distance from their objective. They were now completely encircled by the mobile squadrons of the rebel troops, many of whom were armed with Remington rifles and who were led by the best of the Mahdi's sheikhs. Hicks's army got no farther.

The Dervish attacks spread themselves over three days, and the tired, parched, and despairing troops fought most bravely, if without order. On the first day the enemy was driven back, although the loss to the Egyptians was greater than that of the Dervishes. Water was now almost exhausted, and by singular irony, while the General was doing his utmost to dig wells, less than a mile away, unknown to him, was a large reservoir filled by the rains.

One of the European staff, Major Herlth, kept a diary of the march, which later came into the hands of an Austrian priest, Father Joseph Ohrwalder, who, like his compatriot Slatin Pasha, was for years a prisoner of the Mahdi and of his successor. This diary stops abruptly on November 4, 1883, its last entry being:

We are in a forest, and everyone very depressed. The General orders the band to play, hoping that the music may liven us up a little; but the band soon stops, for the bullets are flying from all directions, and camels, mules and men keep dropping down; we are all cramped up together, so the bullets cannot fail to strike. We are faint and weary, and have no idea what to do. . . . The bullets are falling thicker. . . .

III

Three times, in its death agony, the Egyptian army tried to break through the Dervish ranks. Owing to the trees, the guns could not be properly laid, and many were abandoned. Despite the despairing valour shown by the men, discipline was completely gone, and the bodies of those who had perished in the three attacks lay in great heaps extending over a distance of nearly two miles.

At last, on November 5th, the end came. It was swift. Hicks led a final charge in vain. The Dervishes swept upon the remains of the force and killed them with their spears. The General himself was one of the last to fall, and his conduct, and that of the other Europeans, moved even the Mahdi himself to admiration. Having emptied his revolver, and holding his sword in his right hand, Hicks, mounted on a white horse, and with his back to a tree, waited for the rush of the enemy. He was soon surrounded, and his horse wounded from behind. He then dismounted and fought most gallantly with his sword until he fell, pierced by several spears.

Of the officers who fell with him the most notable was undoubtedly Colonel Farquhar, whose personal bravery throughout the march had been magnificent. No quarter was given during the battle, and of the whole army scarcely five hundred men escaped, most of whom were captured later by the Dervishes and dragged in triumph into El Obeid. The enemy, stripping the dead of all they had, afterwards made pyramids of the skulls.

Kashgil was something more than an isolated triumph or a particularly ghastly massacre. It enabled the Mahdi to establish himself as supreme in the Sudan. After his re-entry into El Obeid he was worshipped almost as a god. The long defence of Khartoum and the death of Gordon was still to come, but in effect the Sudan was his and his successors until the reconquest in the campaigns of 1897 and 1898 under Kitchener, which at length ended the years of darkness and death. Kashgil was a political as well as a military disaster.

Visiting the battlefield over twenty years later, Sir Reginald Wingate recorded his opinion that, had the march been conducted "by a far more numerous and efficient force, the

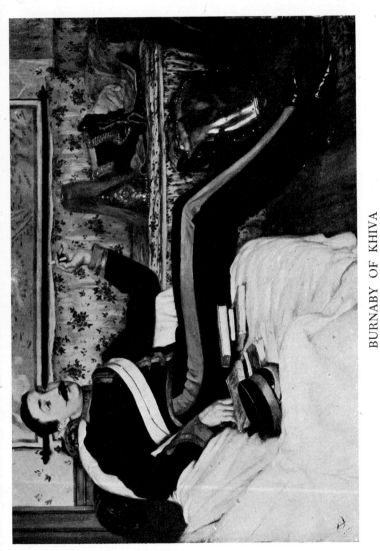

BURNABY OF KHIVA

From a painting by Tissot in the National Portrait Gallery

result would have been the same. It is abundantly evident that the Government of that period neither realized the situation nor appreciated the enormous difficulties attendant on the movement of a large force through such country." Even Colonel Farquhar reproached Hicks bitterly in his note-books (also seen by Slatin) for ever having started on such a campaign with such an army, and indeed, there is little evidence that Hicks possessed any striking power either as leader or organizer.

Of Hicks's personal qualities, his bravery is that which is most clearly without dispute. During the earlier campaign conducted from Khartoum, Colonel Colborne remarked upon his reckless hazard of his own life in reconnaissance work which might reasonably have been left to members of his staff. He also remarked his tact; but in the case of Ala-el-Din Pasha this quality must have deserted him.

While it is agreed that Hicks underestimated the difficulties of the country west of the White Nile; that he placed reliance upon guides whose integrity was far from assured; and that his opinion of the fighting qualities of the Dervish was low, it must be remembered that his experience of the Sudan began with his first successful expedition, and ended with his second. That he had some reason to doubt that the enemy was present in any considerable strength is stated by Ohrwalder, who relates in detail Colonel Farquhar's almost single-handed feats on the march against isolated bodies of the Dervishes. These sallies led him into an almost con-temptuous fearlessness which was shared by most of the European officers, but not, unhappily, by the listless, exhausted and thirsty troops, to whom the Sudan itself was hated exile.

The accounts of the actual numbers opposing Hicks have been varyingly estimated. It is certain that Gordon's idea of 4,000, as recorded in his Journals, is far from the truth. Most authorities agree in putting the figure at about 40,000;

and for the slaughter of Kashgil the Mahdi himself was careful to take the principal glory.

If Hicks is to-day comparatively forgotten, the story of his personal bravery is fine, if tragic. He has some memorial in the grim relics of Kashgil, which include a Nordenfeldt gun captured by the Mahdi, still to be seen in the Khalifa's house at Omdurman. It may also be said that, out of this disaster, and that of Gordon which swiftly followed it, there ultimately came under the protection of Great Britain a vast country whose present peace and prosperity are in contrast to the dark history of preceding centuries.

21

BURNABY OF KHIVA

WHEN the painter Tissot wished to portray a guards-
man hero, he chose, very sensibly, Frederick
Burnaby of The Blues. Burnaby was then a captain,
and the author of a best seller. The artist shows him reclining
on a sofa, smoking a cigarette, with books and a forage cap
littering the space at his side. In the background is a large
wall map, while beneath it, on another sofa, is the impedi-
menta of a full-dress uniform, helmet and cuirass being
prominent. Even in so languid a pose, Burnaby's gigantic
size, his grace and his air of power are astonishing. Here,
one feels, is not a type but an individual, perhaps even an
eccentric. The effect is heightened by the man's pallid complexion, an inheritance, he used to say, from his remote
ancestor King Edward I, which contrasts almost dramatically
with his large black moustache and his bold, lazy eyes.
Burnaby was twenty-eight at the time of the portrait, which
is in many ways felicitous, for not only does it show posterity
his appearance as he was in his prime, but in later years,
when he began to put on weight too heavily, he seldom
allowed himself either to be painted or photographed,
although the rule was relaxed on occasion. Certainly no
more revealing portrait exists.

Burnaby was born to easy circumstances, and into a
leisurely world. His father was a wealthy squire-parson, a
fox-hunting autocrat whose estates lay in Leicestershire.
Frederick Gustavus was born in 1842, in Bedford, where his
father then had a living. His mother was equally well born,
being one of the three beautiful daughters of Henry Villebois,
of Marham, Norfolk. He was the third child, and the elder
of two sons. The phrase "born with a silver spoon in his

179   *

mouth" seems fit to use of him, if it be added that he was one of the rarer people who, far from making an excuse of fortune, took to the fullest his wide opportunities of carving out a romantic career for himself.

From Bedford Grammar School he went to Harrow, thence to Dresden, to study languages, for which he showed an early aptitude. At the age of seventeen he entered the Royal Horse Guards, passing his examination with great credit, being the youngest candidate. He remained in the army for the rest of his life, eventually becoming commanding officer of his regiment. The Crimea and the Mutiny were over, and the usual complaint among officers of his day was that they lived in times of peace too piping for their own prosperity. This was particularly true of the Regiments of Guards, whose officers, so Burnaby complained in later life, spent a great deal too much time and thought upon their tailors, and even their perfumers, to the neglect of their profession. Burnaby himself, though his interests were widespread, was a keen soldier from the first; an able cavalry officer in an age when to give too much application to the routine of military life was considered in some quarters almost bad form. But Burnaby was never afraid of flouting conventions, good or bad. The one thing he could not stand was to be bored, and, in a time which might for him have been peculiarly devoid of excitement, he managed to crowd into a brief life more incident than most men.

His immense height—he was six foot four, and forty-six inches round the chest—always made him conspicuous, and legends of his muscular strength floated from barrack to drawing-room. As a young man, he kept himself in excellent training; he was a good boxer and fencer, and could beat many professional athletes at their own game. Perhaps the most remarkable story told of him concerns two small ponies which were sent by a foreign potentate as a present to Queen Victoria. Before they were delivered at the castle, a wag thought it would be a good joke to put them in Burnaby's rooms at Windsor. Having driven them up the stairs without much difficulty, it proved perfectly impossible to make them descend. Burnaby himself solved the problem at once. He carried them down an entire flight, one under each arm.

His first enthusiasm, and it was a lasting one, was for ballooning, his initiation taking place in a huge and highly dangerous Montgolfier fire-balloon owned by a Frenchman, M. Jean Godard. This balloon was called the *Eagle*, and was probably the largest pear-shaped aerostat ever constructed. The ascent was made from Cremorne Gardens, Chelsea, and after an adventurous journey, the Thames being three times crossed, Greenwich marshes were reached without mishap. Burnaby then joined the Aeronautical Society, and made many voyages in gas-balloons with such men as Coxwell, Westcar and, later, Wright, in one of whose balloons he made a lone drift across the Channel in 1882, almost immediately after an abortive attempt by Brine and Simmons. He had many narrow escapes, being once in a balloon which burst in mid-air, but which acted as a parachute and broke his descent.

Having had an early taste of life abroad, and being fortunate enough to obtain long leaves of absence, usually in the winter, it is not surprising that Burnaby soon became an experienced traveller. His aptitude for languages was specially useful, and he had two other advantages of which he was not slow to make use—journalistic connections, at first with *Vanity Fair* and later with *The Times*.

Being, in company with many of his time, much occupied with what was then known as the Eastern Question, he took pains to acquire a knowledge of Russian early in his career, although his first protracted excursion abroad was made to France and Spain, in 1869. The year following found him in St. Petersburg, Moscow, and Odessa; while two years later he attended the Prince of Wales to the Vienna Exhibition.

It was in 1873 that he first had the idea of visiting Khiva in Turkestan, an undertaking which he was preparing to make with his equally huge soldier-servant, George Radford of The Blues, whose devotion to Burnaby became a by-word. The pair had got no farther than Naples when Burnaby was struck down with typhoid fever, and was only saved from being brutally turned out of his hotel by the intervention of no less a person than the Duke of Connaught, who happened to be in the town at the time.

The next year found him again in Spain, writing letters to *The Times* from scenes of action of the Carlist War. Radford and his master were actually present at the battles of Allo, Dicastillo, Viana, and Maneru, as well as the siege of Tolosa and the capture of Estella. Burnaby and Don Carlos, both men of vast stature, became friendly, although the development of the war itself was not to Burnaby's taste, and he was glad enough to return to England.

Considering what Winwood Reade rightly called its "obscurity," it will always be remarkable how many of the greater Victorian soldiers and statesmen were linked with the Sudan: Gordon, Stewart, Wilson, Gladstone, Wolseley, Cromer, Kitchener, to name the most obvious alone. Burnaby himself was to pay three memorable visits to that huge country, none of which was in an official capacity. His first was in 1874–75, when, at the request of *The Times*, he went to the Equatorial Provinces to obtain an impression of the work which Gordon was doing as administrator for the Khedive, particularly in the suppression of the slave trade. From Suakin, he travelled to Berber by the desert route, not without adventure, and then, turning south, went up the Nile to Khartoum. He next visited Sobat, where he made the acquaintance of Gordon, and was deeply impressed by his methods of administering justice.

Learning accidentally in Khartoum that the Russians had refused entrance to Europeans into Central Asia, Burnaby definitely decided to visit Khiva and started on his journey on November 30, 1875. In St. Petersburg he was told that he might as well try to get to the moon. He applied for permission to go to India *via* Khiva, Merve, and Cabal, and as no direct obstacles were put in his way by the officials, he went by train to Sizerain and thence travelled by a *troika*, or three-horse sleigh, to Orenberg, in conditions of the most frightful cold. Ursk and Karabootak were next reached and passed, and then came Kasala and the ride across the desert to Khiva. He left Kasala in seventy-two degrees of frost with a Tartar servant, a Turkoman camel driver, a guide, three camels and two horses, and on arriving at Kalenderhana, learned that Khiva could not be entered without permission of the Khan. This was ultimately granted, and the traveller even had a personal interview with the potentate, who was most affable, discussed a possible Russian advance on India, and warned Burnaby that England would soon have to fight the Tsar again.

He next went to Petro-Alexandrovsk, where he found a telegram from the Duke of Cambridge requiring his immediate return to European Russia. "Anyway," was his remark, "I have seen Khiva." On his return home, he at once set about to record his experiences, and his book, *A Ride to Khiva*, was published in the autumn of 1876. It met with a chorus of approval, and within a few months was in its eleventh edition.

While *A Ride to Khiva* cannot be called in any sense a masterpiece, it is not to be despised even as a literary work. It held its own generation in wonder, and it is almost as readable to-day as when it was first written. The trouble is, we know so much more, not merely about Central Asia, but of the subsequent evolution of the problem of the advance of Russia, with which Burnaby, in common with many of his time, was always much concerned. *A Ride to Khiva* was, when it was written, a first-rate topical treatise, as well as a stirring narrative of an adventurous journey. It is the narrative which still commands respect. Burnaby was a graphic writer. He observed, and he recorded well, if without an artist's sense of selection. He made no pretence to being anything more than a journalist, but he was a good one; and the strange and exciting nature of his material lends to his work a permanent freshness and interest which would possibly have surprised its author. If *A Ride to Khiva* is not widely read to-day, it is because so many books with similar attraction have been written since.

The same year as the publication of his book saw the beginning of another memorable journey, made with Radford. This was to Asia Minor. England was at that time passionately indignant over the Bulgarian massacres, and feeling against the Turks ran high. Burnaby, who always liked the Turks, was of the opinion that the atrocities were in part a retaliation for similar cruelties inflicted on the Turkish people by Russians and other Christian races. He determined, therefore, to visit the scene of the trouble and see for himself. Smyrna, Constantinople, Scutari, Angora, Tokat, Egin, Erzeroum, Khoi, and Ardahan were the chief points of his route, made mainly on horseback. After his return he published another book, *On Horseback Through Asia Minor*, for which he was paid an advance of £2,500. Again he had a great success, and was inundated with invitations. Like Gordon, he found it a bore being lionized.

In 1877 the Russo-Turkish War broke out, and in the winter Burnaby obtained the honorary post of travelling agent to the Stafford House Committee, a body of people who sent surgeons and dressers to the seat of war. Again Radford accompanied him. Ultimately he joined Valentine Baker's forces, and was present with him at the battle of Tashkesan, in which he commanded the 5th Turkish Brigade.

Baker, after a distinguished career in the British Army, which had ended abruptly and disastrously, had joined the Turkish service, and greatly distinguished himself as a strategist. The two men were to meet again after this first contact, which incidentally cost Burnaby his servant's life, for Radford, after tender nursing by his master, succumbed in England to the rigours of the winter retreat of the Turkish forces in which they both had taken part.

Not content with war and aeronautics, Burnaby next embarked upon matrimony, with the happiest results; he also tried politics, and attempted the hopeless task of bearding Chamberlain at Birmingham. Hopeless it was; and when asked why he did not try some more easy constituency, he replied, "I never fly at small game. Besides, if I were to win Birmingham, I should be offered a place in the Cabinet!" The Conservatives in the Midland city at that time were in a great minority and highly unpopular.

But for his huge size, Burnaby would several times have been roughly handled by the mob, and, although he did better at the polls than many even of his friends could have hoped, he had no chance of election. The year 1880, if it did not see him in the House of Commons, at least gave him an heir. Marriage made up for what politics lacked, and Burnaby also had the minor political satisfaction of being among the original and most active members of the Primrose League.

In 1884 occurred Burnaby's second visit to the Sudan. Just as the time came round for his annual leave of absence, a telegram arrived from Valentine Baker's wife, asking him to join her husband, now in the service of the Khedive, at Suakin. Burnaby did not hesitate. He had been disappointed at not receiving command of a detachment of The Blues which had seen service in Egypt two years before. Now was his chance for further activity. The Madhi had risen, had annihilated the Egyptian forces under Hicks Pasha, and his able lieutenant, Osman Digna, was menacing the Red Sea littoral. The situation was serious.

Valentine Baker had command of a rabble known as the Egyptian Gendarmerie, and he had been sent by the Egyptian Government against Osman Digna. His men were ill-equipped and ill-disciplined, and at the first battle of El Teb, on February 5th, at which Burnaby was present, his men either surrendered or bolted before the Dervishes, offering no resistance whatever. Burnaby and Baker both had narrow escapes, but both lived to fight, three weeks later, under General Graham at the second and successful battle of the same name, in which both were wounded. Baker had the satisfaction of being in action with the regiment he had formerly commanded, the 10th Hussars, while Burnaby gained some notoriety by his use in action of so curious a weapon as a double-barrelled shot-gun, with which he did much execution. It is typical of all British officers of the time (including Gordon), that even the implications of Hicks's disaster could not make them take the Dervish sufficiently seriously as a fighting man. It was left to Kitchener to appreciate the Sudanese aptitude in war, as the tactics of the River War, many years later, were to show.

Burnaby next returned to political activity in Birmingham with his arm in a sling and a magnificent story for his audience. At first he had a splendid reception. "What a pity," said the Radicals, "that he's a d—d Tory;" and there is no doubt that his popularity as a speaker, with war experience as his theme, reached its height. His plank was, of course, the attitude taken up towards Gordon by Gladstone's Government, and the slowness of the measures to help him. He did his theme justice, and it was perhaps unfortunate that there was at that time no chance of an election. But the tide of public feeling quickly turned, and his last appearances in the Midland city were less happy—indeed, were marked by rioting.

The last scene of all was once more in the Sudan. The expedition to relieve Gordon had been organized at last. Wolseley chose the pick of the Guards and the cavalry to form a camel corps to make a dash across the desert, and Burnaby, who from past services, and from the fact that he was now in command of his own regiment, might have expected to be given command of the Household Cavalry detachment, was again disappointed. Again his winter leave was approaching, and he happened to know that steps were being taken to see that he should not go to the scene of action. He announced, therefore, that he was visiting South Africa, and the authorities promptly wired to the Cape forbidding the officials to allow him to take part in any military operations in that part of the world.

"I suppose," said an old farmer on his estate at Somerby, "you're a-going to the Sudan, Colonel?" Burnaby parried the question. "Be advised and don't go," said the old man. "If an Arab could hit a haystack, he couldn't very well miss you."

If the authorities were not anxious to send him with the expedition, Wolseley himself, as Commander-in-Chief, was glad enough of his surreptitious arrival, and at once made him inspecting officer of the line between Tanjour and Magrakeh on the Nile, adding him to his Intelligence Staff. There was no question of his value in the campaign. His Arabic was excellent, and he already had at least some knowledge of the forbidding country, and of the conditions of desert fighting.

He was next appointed to the Desert Column under Sir Herbert Stewart, and was killed on January 17, 1885, in a skirmish outside the zeriba at Abou Klea, while on a reconnaissance. In the confusion of battle, he did not fall back in time upon the main forces. He perished, along with Darley, Wolfe, De Lisle, and other equally gallant officers, and was buried almost where he fell. He was in command at the time of the left-rear of the square, performing the duties of a brigadier.

So passed the man known to his contemporaries as "the bravest of the brave," like Ajax, "smitten in the throat." His death was as dramatic as so much of his life had been. He had seen many battles, yet had never been given the supreme privilege to a soldier, of leading his own men into action. His active service was, indeed, almost inconceivably irregular for an officer of The Blues.

In his lifetime, Burnaby had become a legend. His death was mourned universally. It was felt that a hero had passed, one whose exploits had often caused England to wonder: a man often impatient of authority, and endeared by that very trait to the average Englishman. His passions were theirs. He was a man whom they could understand, a simple giant who did so much, and who might, had he lived, have done so much more.

POSTSCRIPT: AFTERNOON TEA

THE cottage garden ran the ten yards between the front door and the gate, on either side of which was a low brick wall, kept scrupulously free from creeper. Mrs. Mellish liked the colour of the brick, and on summer afternoons, towards tea time, the light fell upon the wall and made it warm. Flowers by the path—candytuft, marigolds, canterbury bells, snapdragons, and, along the edge, virginia stock—hid it from the front door, but from the windows of the room, on either side, it could be seen across the grass between the lupins. Passers-by would sometimes run their hands along its smooth top. It gave the garden dignity.

Jacob Mellish was away at the farm, doing the last jobs before cutting the hay, and his wife, knowing that if the weather held she would be in the fields herself for the hay-making within a day or two, was enjoying what little time she still had for her own. She took such a pride in her plot that she believed it the neatest, the best cared for in all Kerryland. Her father had been head gardener at the hall for fifteen years, and she had caught much of his infectious craving for order. Tidy Tilly they used to call her as a girl, but with respect.

In, lift, twist, shake, in again went her light fork, turning the brown earth, dusty on the top from the sun, cool and pungent beneath. She paused, stretched herself, and went indoors to put the kettle on the range in the kitchen. She felt almost ready for a cup of tea and was sorry, for once, to be having it by herself. The kettle filled, she returned through the front room and stood for a moment at her open door, watching the shadow cast by the cottage as the sun, inclining to westward, gradually drove it back.

No one who does not recollect it can imagine without a

conscious effort the quietness of a village merely forty years ago. It had always lapped Mrs. Mellish and her kind. They had known nothing else. Anywhere in her Norfolk garden sounds would tell her, on a windless day, what was happening in the village on the edge of which her dwelling stood, and in the fields near to it.

Sounds would tell her what Jacob might be doing. The clip-clop of a horse and the pace and particular rumble of wheels revealed who was on the move on the dusty high-road. The ring of iron from the forge told her whether the smith was shoeing or making an iron tyre. And the trains, ambling through the shallow cutting beyond the hill, came by at such regular times that a clock was almost superfluous. Approaching the curve to the level-crossing, the driver would whistle twice, so that even inside the house Mrs. Mellish would know when it was five to ten, or three fifteen, or five, or seven of an evening. The motor was existent, but it had not yet confused the clear and regular sounds which told so much.

Yet even as she stood before her door Mrs. Mellish heard the tentative approach of an ancestor of those machines which would so change the land. It was not the spluttering racket of the doctor's coupé, but a stranger, quieter noise altogether—that of a chain-driven limousine. It was coming from the Norwich direction but it never reached the end of her wall. A sudden pis-s-s-h, a pause in the sound of the transmission, the g-r-r-r of the brakes, and the car had halted. Standing on tiptoe, she could just see the front of the roof, where there was a rack for spare tyres and for luggage. The driver pulled neatly into the side of the road, the engine stopped, and the only sounds now were the quiet voices of men as they clambered up the side of the car to unstrap a spare tyre, and began the serious business of jacking.

Mrs. Mellish was not as a rule interested in motors, which

still rather scared her, but this one was so large that curiosity drove her to the gate, just as it had driven the grey mare on the opposite side of the road to lean over her hedge and whinny. Two liveried men were attending to the trouble; one gentleman in a tall hat was standing beside them, and in the back of the car a fourth man remained seated. He had a beard. He sat where Mrs. Mellish could just see him, smoking.

There was something else wrong beside a puncture, and the work proceeded—in a very orderly way too, thought Mrs. Mellish. Not like the way the doctor did things. He would swear at the least trouble, and seemed more often under his little car than in it. After a few minutes the bearded man got out too, and stood with his own tall hat shining beside that of his friend.

In the kitchen the kettle began to sing. Mrs. Mellish thought of it, though she could not hear it, and it decided her.

She opened the gate.

"P'raps," she called to the two gentlemen, "p'raps you could do with a cup of tea this hot day?"

"Very good idea too," came in a resonant voice from the beard. He left his companion standing with the mechanics, while his own dignified bulk approached his hostess.

". . . the other gentlemen too?"

"Oh," said the man, and his eyes twinkled, "the others will find everything they want in the car. That is, if you can do just with me?"

"With pleasure, I'm sure," said Mrs. Mellish, as she led the way towards her front room.

It was, she thought, "just with him," for his presence seemed to fill her cottage. He was barely able to sit in her largest chair, though once ensconced it seemed to fit him like a glove. Presently she was darting in and out with teacups, bread and butter, honey, cherry jam, and some rock cakes of yesterday's baking.

The man eyed her shrewdly, almost imperiously, before folding his legs comfortably beneath him. He then settled down to the business at hand. Mrs. Mellish, strictly speaking, had meant a cup of tea; she had not expected the huge zest with which her visitor tackled everything she produced from her cupboard.

"My! you must be hungry!" she said. "Have you come far?"

The eyes looked surprised, and at first a little angry; then they smiled. "Well, if you *will* produce such nice things of course I must eat them. And as for coming far, yes, beyond Norwich. We've a long way to go back too."

"I think if you'll excuse me I will just see how the other gentlemen are getting on."

"You needn't worry, I assure you, Mrs. ——"

"Mellish."

"Mrs. Mellish. I give you my word that they will be perfectly happy. You can hear them now—that's the hand-pump they are using. They'll soon have that tyre right and the other adjustment made, and then they'll have a snack before we start off again. I always have something ready in the car in case of breakdowns, but I couldn't resist your very kind suggestion."

Mrs. Mellish thought he did indeed look the kind of man who would not refuse anything which lay in the power of her sex to offer.

"Troublesome things them motors must be," she said.

"Perhaps. But they are great fun for all that, and you'll see, they'll be all over these Norfolk roads one day."

"I hope they won't, if you'll excuse my saying so. They're too noisy altogether."

"Noisy? Why, do you know, Mrs. Mellish, my companion and I are able to talk quite easily at the back of my car, when we are whirling along sometimes at over thirty miles an hour."

"And the dust, too! When one of the bigger cars come by there's a regular whirlwind in the lane, and it blows all over my garden."

"I'm sorry for that. It's such a pretty little garden too."

"I'm glad you think so, sir, for I'm right proud of it...."

"You may well be."

"Another cup?"

"Just one more if I may. It's very refreshing."

As she handed him his last cup the visitor produced a leather case from his pocket, and for one moment Mrs. Mellish thought he was going to discuss payment. But it was a cigar he wanted, and without asking her leave he puffed a big cloud of the rich smoke into the room. What Jacob would think she couldn't imagine. She herself had never smelt a cigar before. She was glad the window was wide open, and that she was the other side of the room.

The visitor cleared his throat and leant back at his ease. Mrs. Mellish began to wonder when she would be rid of him, though his talk was so pleasant and complimentary that she checked the thought at once.

Presently the other gentleman, leaving the car, opened the gate and walked up the brick path.

"All right, Wintrington," called the visitor, "I'll rejoin you immediately."

He was as good as his word. He heaved his majestic bulk from the chair, turned to his hostess, and with a graciousness which she found quite natural, if a little over-whelming, thanked her for her "sumptuous tea." As he climbed into the car she heard him give a hearty laugh, and hoped that it was at some remark made by his companion, not at her. She stood at the gate, and as the grating gears engaged and the shining car swept on its way she was reassured by a lifting of the tall hat, a wave of the hand, and a smile of what she felt to be real friendliness.

The first thing she did when she returned to the cottage

was to brush the cigar ash from the floor and to open the
door at the back to let a draught through the house.

Jacob noticed nothing, but in reciting the news of the
day over the supper table remarked that it was surprising
he should have chosen to come through Kerryland, and
even past this very cottage.

"Did you see him pass, Tilly?"

"Why who, Jacob?" said Mrs. Mellish.

"Haven't you heard? Goods train held him up at the
level-crossing, and signalman recognized him sitting in the
back of the motor with one of his gentlemen. Crown on
the panel of the doors too, so he said. Why, t'was
King Edward!"

NOTE

To compile a list of the many standard works which have been consulted would be tedious and unnecessary; but some record of other sources is given below. The dates of editions are of those read, not necessarily of the first.

I. *Threnodia Carolina:* Sir Thomas Herbert (1678, and with additional matter concerning the King's burial, 1813).

II. *The Great Lord Fairfax:* Sir Clements Markham (1875).

The Lord General: M. A. Gibb (1938).

Poems and Letters of Andrew Marvell: H. M. Margoliouth (1927).

Andrew Marvell: M. C. Bradbrook and M. G. Lloyd Thomas (1940).

Fairfax MSS.: Bodleian.

III. *Life of Monck:* Thomas Gumble (1671).

Observations upon Military and Political Affairs: Monck (1671).

Honest George Monck: J. D. Griffith Davies (1936).

IV. Pepys, here as elsewhere.

Cromwell's Understudy: W. H. Dawson (1938).

V. *Lives of the Regicides:* Mark Noble (1798).

VI. *An Exact Accompt of the . . . Trial of Twenty-Nine Regicides* (1660).

VII. *Essays and Orations:* Sir Henry Halford (1833).

Cromwell's Burial: C. R. Haines (1927).

VIII. *The Protectorate House of Cromwell:* Mark Noble (1784).

Numismata Cromwelliana: H. W. Henfrey (1887).

IX. Publications of the Navy Record Society.

X. *Life of Hawke:* Montagu Burrows (1883).

XI. *Original Hymns and Poems* by Philotheorus (1777). Minutes of the Court Marshal on the Loss of the *Royal George:* Record Office, Adm. 1/5321.

 Narrative of the Loss of the "Royal George" (1842).

 The British Navy in Adversity: W. M. James (1926).

XII. *Admiral Duncan:* Earl of Camperdown (1898).

XIII. *Life and Letters of Admiral Cornwallis:* G. Cornwallis West (1927).

XIV. *Blackwood's Magazine,* July 1833.

XV. *Narrative of the Services of H.M.S. "Superb":* J. S. Tucker (1838).

XVI. *Life of a Sailor:* Frederick Chamier (1850).

XVII. Contemporary Lives by Watkins, Wright, Huish.

 The Patriot King: Grace E. Thompson (1932).

XVIII. *Diary:* William Dyott, ed. R. W. Jeffery (1907).

XIX. *Our Heroes of the Crimea:* George Ryan (1855).

XX. *With Hicks Pasha in the Soudan:* J. Colborne (1884).

XXI. *A Ride to Khiva* (1877).

 Life of Burnaby: Mann (1882).